Data Visualization Made Simple

D0879814

Data Visualization Made Simple is a practical guide to the fundamentals, strategies, and real-world cases for data visualization, an essential skill required in today's information-rich world. With foundations rooted in statistics, psychology, and computer science, data visualization offers practitioners in almost every field a coherent way to share findings from original research, big data, learning analytics, and more.

In nine appealing chapters, the book:

- examines the role of data graphics in decision making, sharing information, sparking discussions, and inspiring future research;
- scrutinizes data graphics, deliberates on the messages they convey, and looks at options for design visualization; and
- includes cases and interviews to provide a contemporary view of how data graphics are used by professionals across industries.

Both novices and seasoned designers in education, business, and other areas can use this book's effective, linear process to develop data visualization literacy and promote exploratory, inquiry-based approaches to visualization problems.

Kristen Sosulski is Associate Professor of Information Systems and the Director of Learning Sciences for the W.R. Berkley Innovation Labs at New York University's Stern School of Business, USA.

Data Visualization Made Simple

Insights into Becoming Visual

Kristen Sosulski

Routledge
Taylor & Francis Group

NEW YORK AND LONDON

First published 2019
by Routledge
711 Third Avenue, New York, NY 10017

and by Routledge
2 Park Square, Milton Park, Abingdon, Oxon, OX14 4RN

Routledge is an imprint of the Taylor & Francis Group, an informa business

Library of Congress Cataloging-in-Publication Data
A catalog record for this title has been requested

ISBN: 978-1-138-50387-8 (hbk)
ISBN: 978-1-138-50391-5 (pbk)
ISBN: 978-1-315-14609-6 (ebk)

Typeset in Avenir Next
by Apex CoVantage, LLC

For Penn

Contents

Preface

Data visualization is the process of representing information graphically. Relationships, patterns, similarities, and differences are encoded through shape, color, position, and size. These visual representations of data can make your findings and ideas stand out.

Data visualization is an essential skill in our data-driven world. Almost every aspect of our daily routine generates data: the steps we take, the movies we watch, the goods we purchase, and the conversations we have. Much of this data, our digital exhaust, is stored waiting for someone to make sense of it. But why is anyone interested in these quotidian actions?

Imagine you are Nike, Netflix, Amazon, or Twitter. Your data helps these companies better understand you and other users like you. Companies utilize this information to target markets, develop new products, and ultimately outpace their competition by knowing their customers' habits and needs. However, such insights do not just "automagically" happen.

One does not simply transform data into information. It requires several steps: cleaning the data, formatting the data, interrogating the data, analyzing the data, and evaluating the results.

Let's take this a step further. Suppose you identify new markets your company should target. Would you know how to effectively share this information? Could you provide clear evidence that would convince your company to allocate resources to implement your recommendations?

What would you rather present: a spreadsheet with the raw data? Or a graphic that shows the data analyzed in an informative way? I imagine you would want to show your insight so that it could be understood by anyone from interns to executives.

Data visualization can help make access to data equitable. Data graphics with dashboard displays and/or web-based interfaces, can change an organization's culture regarding data use. Access to shared information can promote data-driven decision making throughout the organization.

Clear information presentations that support decision making in your organization can give you a leg up. Understanding data and making it clear for others via data graphics is the art of becoming visual.

The strategies in this book show you how to present clear evidence of your findings to your intended audience and tell engaging data stories through data visualization.

This book is written as a textbook for creatives, educators, entrepreneurs, and business leaders in a variety of industries. The data visualization field is rooted in statistics, psychology, and computer science, which makes it a practice in almost every field that involves data exploration and presentation. Whether you are a seasoned visualization designer or a novice, this book will serve as a primer and reference to becoming visual with data.

As a professor of information systems, my work lies at the intersection of technology, data, and business. I use data graphics in my practice for data exploration and presentation.

I teach executives, full-time MBA students, and train companies in the process of visualizing data. Teaching allows me to stay current with the latest software and challenges me to articulate the key concepts, techniques, and practices needed to become visual. The following chapters embody my data visualization practice and my course curriculum.

This book promotes both an exploratory and an inquiry-based approach to visualization. Data tasks are treated as visualization problems, and they use quantitative techniques from statistics and data mining to detect patterns and trends. You'll learn how to create clear, purposeful, and beautiful displays. Exercises accompany each chapter. This allows you to practice and apply the techniques presented.

How and why do professionals incorporate data visualization into their practice? To answer these questions, I engaged professionals in business analytics, human resources, marketing, research, education, politics, gaming, entrepreneurship, and project management to share their practice through brief case studies and interviews. The cases and interviews illustrate how people and organizations use data visualization to aid in their decision making, data exploration, data modeling, presentation, and reporting. My hope is that these diverse examples motivate you to make data visualization part of your practice.

By the end of this book, you will be able to create data graphics and use them with purpose.

How to Use This Book

This book is intended for use as a textbook on data visualization–the process of creating data graphics. There are five icons that will prompt you to try out a technique, learn more about a practice or topic, and show you how data visualization is used in organizations or one's profession.

Try It

Tutorials and exercises to guide you in becoming visual.

Pro Tip

Short-cuts and best practices from the field.

Sidebar

Additional resources to further your knowledge.

Use Case

An illustration of how data graphics are used in a specific field explained by a practitioner.

Interview With a Practitioner

 Interviewer   Interviewee

Interviews with professionals who use data visualization in their work.

I

BECOMING VISUAL

This chapter answers the following questions:

What is data visualization?
Who are the visualization designers and what do they do?
Why use data visualization?
How can I incorporate data visualization into practice?

Data Visualization Made Simple: Insights into Becoming Visual is a contemporary view of how data graphics are used by professionals across industries. The book examines the role of data graphics in decision making, informing processes, sharing information, sparking discussions, and inspiring future research. It scrutinizes data graphics, deliberates on the message they convey, and looks at design visualizations.

Beautiful (and not so beautiful) charts and graphs are everywhere. Visualization of information is a human practice dating back to the Chauvet cave drawings, over 32,000 years ago (Christianson, 2012). The way we view everyday information, such as the weather, fitness progress, and account balances, is through visual interfaces. These interfaces aggregate and display key data points such as the temperature, calories burned, miles run, and personal rates of return. The charts we regularly use to show quantities and change over time, like bar charts and line graphs, were first employed in the late 1700s.

William Playfair (1786) is credited as the pioneer who showed economic data using bar charts. Playfair (1786) also invented the line graph. Playfair's work in the 1700s is paramount to the field of data visualization; it provided the foundation for future statistical data displays.

Forces of Change

Data visualization has gained immense popularity over the last five years. Many forces have contributed to the torrent of data graphics that we see all around us. First, there's a lot more data available in the world; we are living in the era of big data. From individuals to governments, there is a movement toward sharing data for public good. Platforms like Kaggle provide open data sets and a community to explore data, write and share code, and enter Machine Learning competitions. All of the services we employ, from AT&T to American Express, collect, mine, and share our data. Second, software to analyze and visualize data is ubiquitous. Tableau, for example, is designed for the explicit purpose of visualizing data. It's only been available for both Mac and PC users since 2014. Programming languages such as Python and R have packages, such as ggplot2 and plotly, that make the process of data visualization straightforward and manageable, even for non-programmers. Charts are no longer limited to static displays; they are dynamic, interactive, and animated. Third, the cost of hardware is decreasing while computing power is increasing, in line with or perhaps outpacing Moore's Law. Cloud computing has eliminated the barrier to data storage and processing power; it's possible to mine and visualize data without the economic and maintenance burdens. Fourth, education has embraced these technological advances. Top universities have established research centers and launched academic programs in data science, big data, business analytics and other subject-specific variations. These variations include healthcare analytics, learning analytics, sports analytics, and sustainability analytics. Furthermore, in the spirit of knowledge sharing and freemium content, online tutorials on how to do almost anything can be found on You-Tube. For example, you can learn how to build data graphics through online tutorials. These resources complement this book, and I encourage you to explore them.

Trends in Data Visualization—Storytelling

The use of data graphics for *storytelling* is a popular technique employed to engage an audience. When well-designed data graphics are used in presentations, they highlight the key insights or points you want to accentuate. Storytelling is not limited to in-person presentations. Stories can be told through video, web narratives, and even through audience-driven interfaces.

How can we use visuals to tell engaging data stories and provide evidence of findings or insights? A picture may be worth a thousand words, but not all pictures are readable, interpretable, meaningful, or relevant. Figure 1.1 is a preview of three images that support data stories about Manhattan.[1]

Stories can begin with a question or line of inquiry.

Highlighting behaviors > Who's hailing a cab when the clocks strike midnight on New Year's Eve? Map A shows the location of taxi cab customer pickups at 12:00am on January 1, 2016.

Revealing similarities and differences > Where do the most motor vehicle accidents occur in Manhattan? Map B is a point map that shows the locations of each accident during the month of January 2016.

Displaying locations > Where can I pick up free Wi-Fi? Map C shows the location of each Wi-Fi hotspot in Manhattan.

In many TED Talks, presenters use charts to lead the audience through a narrative about an important topic or issue. Skilled presenters rarely show a graph on the screen without providing some context or explanation. Rather, they highlight specific data points for audience examination or they walk the audience through the graph by progressively revealing key data points.

Telling stories with data: Viewing Manhattan

MAP A   MAP B   MAP C

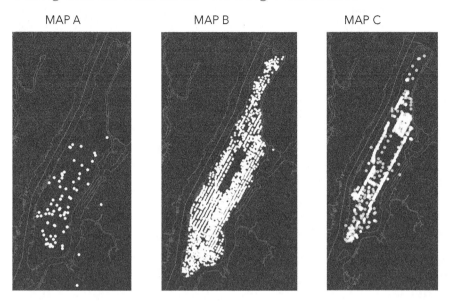

Figure 1.1 Viewing Manhattan through the lens of taxi hails, motor vehicle accidents, and Wi-Fi hotspots.

Examples of presenter-driven storytelling
http://becomingvisual.com/portfolio/presenterdrivenstories

Storytelling does not have to be presenter driven. User-driven storytelling is becoming increasingly popular utilizing data visualizations. For example, the Gapminder Foundation created an interface to view and explore public health data, human development trends and income distribution. The data graphics presented by the *New York Times* allow for rich exploration of the U.S. Census American Time Usage Survey, such as How Different Groups Spend Their Day. Google provides open access to explore Google search trends. With Google Trends, you can compare search volume of different keywords or topics over time. For example, interest in my two alma maters, Columbia University and New York University, is compared over time using a simple line graph. See Figure 1.2.

These are just a few examples of interfaces that are intended to help users build their own stories. Chapters VI–THE AUDIENCE and VII–THE PRESENTATION offer strategies and techniques for delivering presentations and telling stories with data graphics.

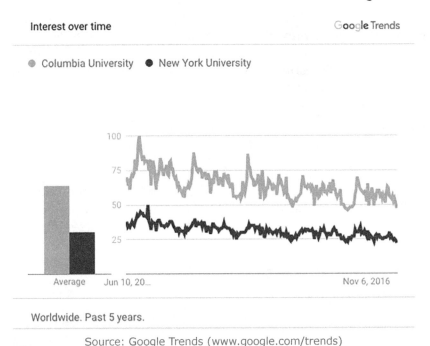

Source: Google Trends (www.google.com/trends)

Figure 1.2 Google search trends for New York University and Columbia University

Examples of user-driven storytelling
http://becomingvisual.com/portfolio/userdrivenstories

Trends in Data Visualization–Interactive Graphics

Static charts and graphics are antiquated. Interactive data graphics are the new norm. This has changed the way we interact with data. From media sites to individual blogs, interactive data graphics are used to engage and entice audiences. Users interact with graphics and search for meaning in the visual information presented, in essence creating their own narrative or story.

Data graphics with filters enable the querying or questioning data through a simple click of a button. The simplicity of visual interfaces that overlay data encourage inquiry without sophisticated training in data science or analytics. The ubiquity of these interfaces impels anyone who works with data to consider interactive data graphics as their new standard format.

Let's use a simple example of how interactive graphics have changed the way we engage with information. Let's say you wanted to know the median household income for your neighborhood. Let's assume you live in trendy Williamsburg, Brooklyn, 11211. How would you expect to be presented with the data?

THE MEDIAN HOUSEHOLD INCOME FOR WILLIAMSBURG, BROOKLYN, 11211 IS $50,943

This information is less than satisfying.

This is the middle household income value for all of the households in 11211. What you may really want to know is the distribution of household income in your neighborhood. The map below (see Figure 1.3)

The boundary of the zip code 11211 in Williamsburg, Brooklyn

Source: *Leaflet* | Data, imagery and map information provided by *CartoDB*, *OpenStreetMap*, and contributors, *CC-BY-SA*

Figure 1.3 A choropleth map showing the boundary of Williamsburg (11211) defined by the green line

outlines Williamsburg in green. Within this neighborhood, there are many U.S. Census Block Groups[2] that are shaded using a grayscale. The darker the shade, the higher the median household income for that particular block group. This allows for comparisons of one census block to another.

Using the city-data.com website, you can highlight those blocks that have the highest and lowest median income by zooming in and selecting specific Census Block Groups.

Figure 1.4 shows the maximum median income for the area and Figure 1.5 shows the minimum.

These three maps show the median income for Williamsburg, Brooklyn in the context of others, rather a single number. The shading in all three maps in Figures 1.3, 1.4, and 1.5 designates the areas with higher (darker shades) versus lower (lighter shades) median household income.

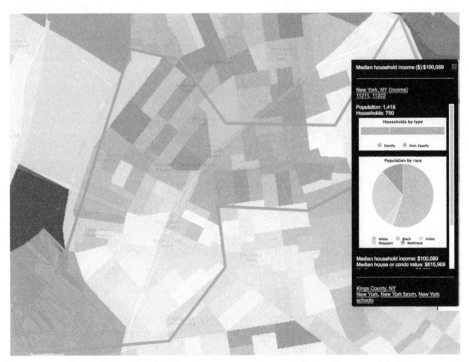

Source: *Leaflet* | Data, imagery, and map information provided by *CartoDB*, *OpenStreetMap*, and contributors, *CC-BY-SA*

Figure 1.4 A Census Block Group (selected in green) has one of the highest median household incomes ($100,089).

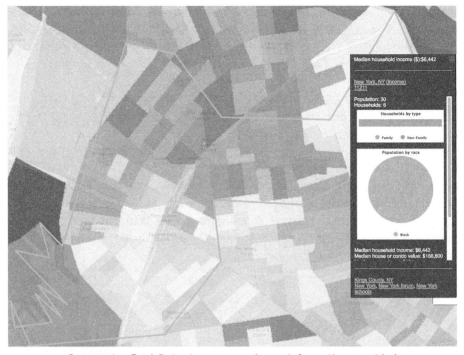

Source: *Leaflet* | Data, imagery, and map information provided
by *CartoDB*, *OpenStreetMap*, and contributors, *CC-BY-SA*

Figure 1.5 A Census Block Group (selected in green) has one of the lowest median household incomes ($6,442).

1.1 What Is Data Visualization?

In my experience, everyone defines this term slightly differently. Let's imagine that you are one of my data visualization graduate students. Before the course begins, I ask my students to define data visualization in their own words.

 I encourage you to quickly take this survey to assess for yourself what you already know about data visualization at: http://becomingvisual.com/survey. Throughout this book, the examples from the survey will be referenced and explained.

On the first day of class, I display a word cloud of student definitions as shown in Figure 1.6. This image depicts the frequency of the top

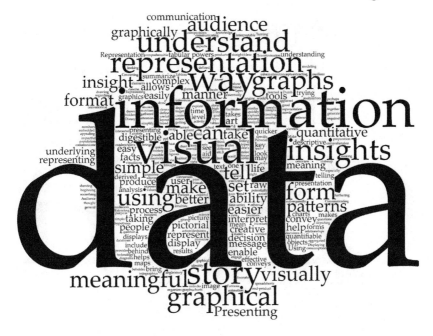

Figure 1.6 A word cloud that shows the frequency of the top 150 words used by students when asked to define data visualization

150 words from their definitions. The larger the word, the more times students used it in a definition. Note: The phrase "data visualization" has been filtered out.

Next, I reduce the list of words from 150 to 40 and re-graph it (see Figure 1.7). The words *data* and *information* stand out as the largest words. Then, we discuss the importance of transforming data into information.

Finally, I reduce the word cloud to the top five words (see Figure 1.8).

This brings us to the key words that comprise the definition: **a visual way to tell a story with data and information.** This exercise always leads to an interesting conversation about how visualization is used in practice.

I conclude this exercise by sharing a few simple explanations by experts in the field.

Visualization is a graphical representation of some data or concepts.

–COLIN WARE, 2008, p. 20

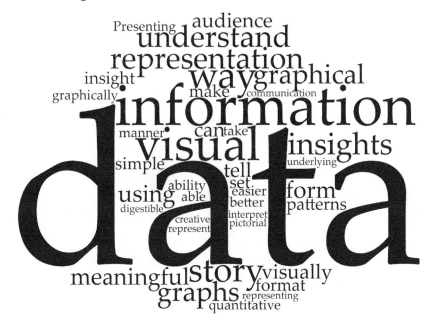

Figure 1.7 A word cloud that shows the frequency of the top 40 words used by students when asked to define data visualization

Figure 1.8 A word cloud that shows the frequency of the top five words used by students when asked to define data visualization

When a chart is presented properly, information just flows to the viewer in the clearest and most efficient way. There are no extra layers of colors, no enhancements to distract us from the clarity of the information.

–DONA WONG, 2010, p. 13

Visualization is a kind of narrative, providing a clear answer to a question without extraneous details.

–BEN FRY, 2008, p. 4

Visualization is often framed as a medium for storytelling. The numbers are the source material, and the graphs are how you describe the source.

—NATHAN YAU, 2013, p. 261

While some view data visualization as a technique, I define data visualization as a **process used to create data graphics**.

1.2 Who Are Visualization Designers and What Do They Do?

Anyone who works with data and visualizes it is a visualization designer. To produce a graphical representation of data, the designer engages in a process where the data is the input, the output is a graphic, and in between is a transformation of data into *an information graphic*. The transformation stage involves chart creation and refinement. After the graphic is refined, it becomes a communication device for use with a target audience.

This book will help you master the practice of data visualization design, whether you are just starting out, or have been working at it for a while. Given that you are reading this book, you may already have some visual instincts. For example, you may cringe when you see a slide presentation with a lot of text or become frustrated when you cannot find the information you need on a poorly designed website. Even if you think that you are not a visual person, you can still visualize data.

Becoming visual means you must develop a new habit.

Habit is a fixed tendency or pattern of behavior that is often repeated and is acquired by one's own experience or learning, whereas an instinct tends to be similar in nature to habit, but it is acquired naturally without any formal training, instruction or personal experience.

DIFFERENCE BETWEEN HABIT AND INSTINCT, 2017, para. 1

Essentially, this means you must integrate visualization into your workflow, rather than making it an extra step in the exploration, analysis and communication of information.

Developing a visual habit requires practice. This book provides many opportunities for such practice. There are conceptual and hands-on exercises at the end of each chapter. No amount of observing or reading will give you competence in visualizing information. The software available makes the actual creation of charts and graphs easy. However, the software will not fix bad data or provide you with worthwhile insights.

The exercises are designed to build your confidence in visualizing data. In addition, you can find visualization tutorials and real examples at becomingvisual.com.

1.3 Why Use Data Visualization?

Over the years, I've given numerous talks on data visualization to students, executives, and data gurus. In my experience, at first, most people want to learn how to best use the tools (see Chapter II—THE TOOLS). However, there is much more to the practice of visualization. There are several arguments for why data visualization is essential to your practice.

 Reason one: to communicate

When data attributes are simplified into a visual language, patterns and trends can reveal themselves for easy comprehension. At the most fundamental level, a table of numbers is useful to look up a single value.

For example, what if you ran a product review site and wanted to know how many daily user reviews were written in a year? Table 1.1 makes it easy to see the total number of reviews by day. On January 4, there were 12 reviews.

How did you read this table of numbers? You probably read each value, individually, one at a time. However, a graph can help us see many values at once. For example, Figure 1.9 shows the number of daily reviews for a single year. You can see how the reviews have fluctuated over time, during each day of each month.

Visual displays combine many values into shapes that we can easily see as a whole, such as the line in the graph that shows the changing number of reviews over time. This enables efficient human information processing because many values can be perceived through a single line (Evelson, 2015), as illustrated in Figure 1.9.

Table 1.1 A table of data that shows the number of user reviews of products by day

Date	Total Reviews
1/2/2018	3
1/3/2018	27
1/4/2018	12
1/5/2018	23
1/6/2018	1
1/7/2018	0
1/8/2018	253
1/9/2018	238
1/10/2018	145

Daily reviews

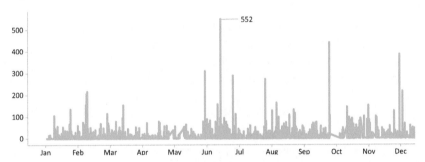

Figure 1.9 A line chart showing daily reviews for a single year

The goal of visualization is to aid our understanding of data by leveraging the human visual system's highly tuned ability to see patterns, spot trends, and identify outliers.

　　　　　　–HEER, Bostock, & Ogievetsky, 2010, p. 1

The arrangement of the data encodings (dots, lines, bars, shaded areas, bubbles, etc.) can reveal where the obvious correlations, relationships, anomalies, or patterns exist. For example, the chart on the left in Figure 1.10 shows a positive correlation while the chart on the right shows the presence of an outlier in the top right corner.

 Reason two: transform data into information

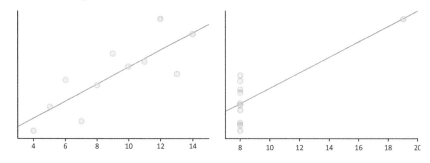

Figure 1.10 A chart showing correlation and outliers based on Anscombe (1973)

In this era of big data, visualization is a powerful way to make sense of the data. Big data is much more than just a lot of data. IBM data scientists break big data into four dimensions: volume, variety, velocity, and veracity.

Data differs with respect to its volume or physical size. This is measured in bytes, the speed in which it is generated (velocity), the forms it takes (variety), and its accuracy (veracity). These differences make data a challenge to work with but provide a terrific opportunity for data exploration.

Learn more about Big Data:
http://becomingvisual.com/portfolio/bigdata

Think about the data you generate every day. For example, when you browse the web, all of your clickstreams and analytics are captured and collected on each page you view. All of your browsing history is saved in your web browser. When you call or text, that history is saved too. Every post, like, view, and click on each online platform from Facebook to Yelp is collected. This collected data is used by companies and researchers to learn more about how people interact (buy, sell, search, communicate, etc.) in online communities.

When it comes to the practical use of data visualization, there is a big difference between using real data to reflect real-world phenomena and the analytical process of modeling to make predictions. In the analysis phase, the data is interrogated to learn more, such as developing an understanding of the particular phenomenon. Then, by identifying a key insight, you can take the data a step further by **transforming a basic information graphic into a knowledge graphic**. To decode the data into usable knowledge requires use of appropriate models, statistics, and data mining techniques for data analysis. Once you make sense of the data insights, you may need to share them with others. This means you must communicate the results in a way that your audience can understand.

> Now, through ADV [Advanced Data Visualization], potential exists for nontraditional and more visually rich approaches, especially in regard to more complex (i.e., thousands of dimensions or attributes) or larger (i.e., billions of rows) data sets, to reveal insights not possible through conventional means.
>
> –EVELSON, 2011, para. 6

The challenge in working with a lot of data is that it can be difficult to view and interpret. For example, on my MacBook Air, I can only view 45 rows of data at any given time with a maximum of 20 attributes (columns) (see Figure 1.11).

Data visualization tools work within the limits of the screen to present data via an interface. The interface may include tools to question, filter, and explore the data visually. With modern software, visualizations can be configured to show deep and broad data sets (see Chapter IV–THE DATA). In addition, they can accommodate data that is dynamic and

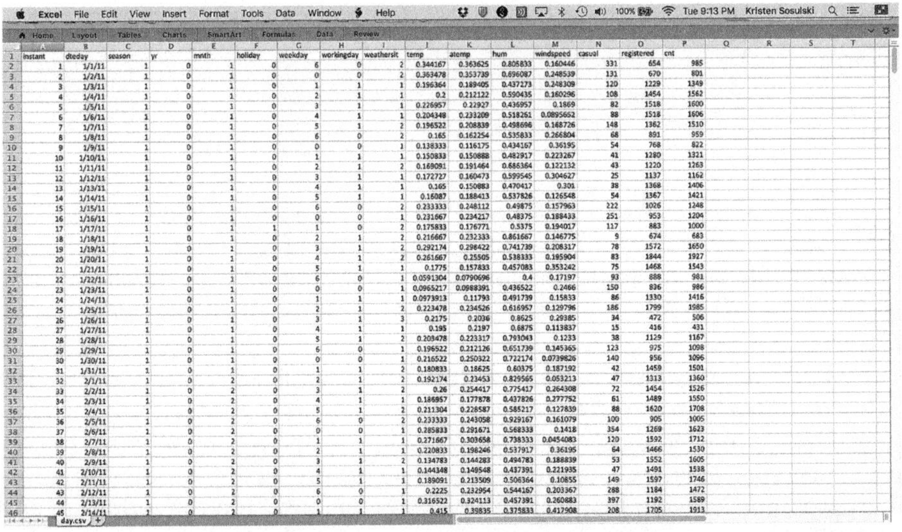

instant	dteday	season	yr	mnth	holiday	weekday	workingday	weathersit	temp	atemp	hum	windspeed	casual	registered	cnt
1	1/1/11	1	0	1	0	6	0	2	0.344167	0.363625	0.805833	0.160446	331	654	985
2	1/2/11	1	0	1	0	0	0	2	0.363478	0.353739	0.696087	0.248539	131	670	801
3	1/3/11	1	0	1	0	1	1	1	0.196364	0.189405	0.437273	0.248309	120	1229	1349
4	1/4/11	1	0	1	0	2	1	1	0.2	0.212122	0.590435	0.160296	108	1454	1562
5	1/5/11	1	0	1	0	3	1	1	0.226957	0.22927	0.436957	0.1869	82	1518	1600
6	1/6/11	1	0	1	0	4	1	1	0.204348	0.233209	0.518261	0.0895652	88	1518	1606
7	1/7/11	1	0	1	0	5	1	2	0.196522	0.208839	0.498696	0.168726	148	1362	1510
8	1/8/11	1	0	1	0	6	0	2	0.165	0.162254	0.535833	0.266804	68	891	959
9	1/9/11	1	0	1	0	0	0	1	0.138333	0.116175	0.434167	0.36195	54	768	822
10	1/10/11	1	0	1	0	1	1	1	0.150833	0.150888	0.482917	0.223267	41	1280	1321
11	1/11/11	1	0	1	0	2	1	2	0.169091	0.191464	0.686364	0.122132	43	1220	1263
12	1/12/11	1	0	1	0	3	1	1	0.172727	0.160473	0.599545	0.304627	25	1137	1162
13	1/13/11	1	0	1	0	4	1	1	0.165	0.150883	0.470417	0.301	38	1368	1406
14	1/14/11	1	0	1	0	5	1	1	0.16087	0.188413	0.537826	0.126548	54	1367	1421
15	1/15/11	1	0	1	0	6	0	2	0.233333	0.248112	0.49875	0.157963	222	1026	1248
16	1/16/11	1	0	1	0	0	0	1	0.231667	0.234217	0.48375	0.188433	251	953	1204
17	1/17/11	1	0	1	1	1	0	2	0.175833	0.176771	0.5375	0.194017	117	883	1000
18	1/18/11	1	0	1	0	2	1	2	0.216667	0.232333	0.861667	0.146775	9	674	683
19	1/19/11	1	0	1	0	3	1	2	0.292174	0.298422	0.741739	0.208317	78	1572	1650
20	1/20/11	1	0	1	0	4	1	2	0.261667	0.25505	0.538333	0.195904	83	1844	1927
21	1/21/11	1	0	1	0	5	1	1	0.1775	0.157833	0.457083	0.353242	75	1468	1543
22	1/22/11	1	0	1	0	6	0	1	0.0591304	0.0790696	0.4	0.17197	93	888	981
23	1/23/11	1	0	1	0	0	0	1	0.0965217	0.0988391	0.436522	0.2466	150	836	986
24	1/24/11	1	0	1	0	1	1	1	0.0973913	0.11793	0.491739	0.15833	86	1330	1416
25	1/25/11	1	0	1	0	2	1	2	0.223478	0.234526	0.616957	0.129796	186	1799	1985
26	1/26/11	1	0	1	0	3	1	3	0.2175	0.2036	0.8625	0.29385	34	472	506
27	1/27/11	1	0	1	0	4	1	1	0.195	0.2197	0.6875	0.113837	15	416	431
28	1/28/11	1	0	1	0	5	1	2	0.203478	0.223317	0.793043	0.1233	38	1129	1167
29	1/29/11	1	0	1	0	6	0	1	0.196522	0.212126	0.651739	0.145365	123	975	1098
30	1/30/11	1	0	1	0	0	0	1	0.216522	0.250322	0.722174	0.0739826	140	956	1096
31	1/31/11	1	0	1	0	1	1	2	0.180833	0.18625	0.60375	0.187192	42	1459	1501
32	2/1/11	1	0	2	0	2	1	2	0.192174	0.23453	0.829565	0.053213	47	1313	1360
33	2/2/11	1	0	2	0	3	1	2	0.26	0.254417	0.775417	0.264308	72	1454	1526
34	2/3/11	1	0	2	0	4	1	1	0.186957	0.177878	0.437826	0.277752	61	1489	1550
35	2/4/11	1	0	2	0	5	1	2	0.211304	0.228587	0.585217	0.127839	88	1620	1708
36	2/5/11	1	0	2	0	6	0	2	0.233333	0.243058	0.929167	0.161079	100	905	1005
37	2/6/11	1	0	2	0	0	0	1	0.285833	0.291671	0.568333	0.1418	354	1269	1623
38	2/7/11	1	0	2	0	1	1	1	0.271667	0.303658	0.738333	0.0454083	120	1592	1712
39	2/8/11	1	0	2	0	2	1	1	0.220833	0.198246	0.537917	0.36195	64	1466	1530
40	2/9/11	1	0	2	0	3	1	2	0.134783	0.144283	0.494783	0.188839	53	1552	1605
41	2/10/11	1	0	2	0	4	1	1	0.144348	0.149548	0.437391	0.221935	47	1491	1538
42	2/11/11	1	0	2	0	5	1	1	0.189091	0.213509	0.506364	0.10855	149	1597	1746
43	2/12/11	1	0	2	0	6	0	1	0.2225	0.232954	0.544167	0.203367	288	1184	1472
44	2/13/11	1	0	2	0	0	0	1	0.316522	0.324113	0.457391	0.260883	397	1192	1589
45	2/14/11	1	0	2	0	1	1	1	0.415	0.39835	0.375833	0.417908	208	1705	1913

Figure 1.11 An Excel spreadsheet open on a MacBook Air that shows the maximum amount of data that can be viewed at one time on my screen

can work with analysis tools for data interrogation through dashboard interfaces.

 Reason three: to show evidence

Data graphics are used to show findings, new insights, or results. The data graphic serves as the visual evidence presented to the audience. The data graphic makes the evidence clear when it shows an interpretable result such as a trend or pattern. Data graphics are only as good as the insight or message communicated.

Using data graphics as evidence are best understood with an example from the field.

Interview with a practitioner

I interviewed Samantha Feldman from Gray Scalable who described how she uses data graphics to support her work.

 Kristen Sosulski (KS)   **Samantha Feldman (SF)**

KS:

Who are you and what do you do?

SF:

I'm Samantha Feldman, I work for Gray Scalable, a consulting firm that provides human resources consulting for start-ups. Most of our clients have somewhere between 150 and 500 employees, are growing quickly, and hire us to help scale their recruiting practice, train their employees, and provide help with employee relations. I run the reporting and analytics arm of the business. The majority of my client projects center around helping our clients with employee compensation models, recruiting reporting, employee survey analysis, and pretty much any HR practice where numbers are involved.

KS:

How do you use data visualization in your practice?

SF:

The most common question I get from my clients is "how are we paying our employees relative to market rates?" This requires understanding broader market data, employee seniority, different job functions, and a few other variables. Most of our competitors provide results for each employee in spreadsheet format. Reviewing hundreds of rows of information makes it hard to get a holistic understanding of your current pay practices or see trends among different levels or job functions. I use data visualization to solve that, with what one of our clients named "the dot graph."

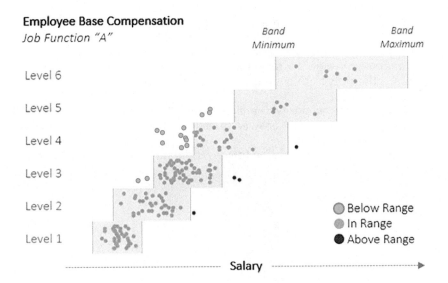

Employee Base Compensation
Job Function "A"

KS:

What insight is evidenced by the graph provided? What did you do with that insight?

SF:

In the graph, every employee is represented by a dot. From this one view, a client (usually the head of operations, finance, or HR) can quickly see that most employees fall within market salary bands.

A visualization like this also helps them spot how large the trouble spots are. In this case, I would point out that employees are being paid within range for the first three levels, but that employees start to fall behind around Levels 4 and 5. These could be employees who have been at the company long enough that their salary increases have not kept pace with the market. They could be underpaid for a number of other reasons (we also look to make sure gender is not a factor). From here, I do a deeper dive with the client to show who those employees are and devise a plan to correct employee compensation where needed.

KS:

How did you create it? What was that data? What was the software? What would have been the alternative?

SF:

This graph was created with Tableau. It starts as a box and whisker plot—with the box and whisker reference lines removed. In their place, I make a reference band that is unique to each level and job function. One of the more important things I figured out how to do is to add a jitter calculation in Tableau (the reason the dots look scattered within the level). Because a company can have a group of employees that all make the same salary (e.g., 10 account managers who all make $65,000), this keeps the dots from overlapping and allows you to see the true volume of employees.

When I am on site with a client doing this with Tableau, I set up the tooltip so I can easily answer questions about specific employees as well, as shown below.

The alternative would be to view the data as a table by employee:

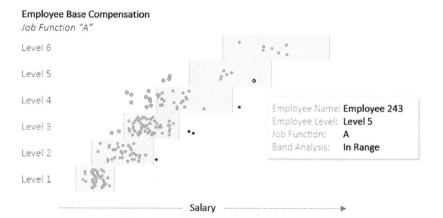

Employee Base Compensation
Job Function "A"

Level 6
Level 5
Level 4
Level 3
Level 2
Level 1

Employee Name: **Employee 243**
Employee Level: **Level 5**
Job Function: **A**
Band Analysis: **In Range**

Salary

				Salary range in USD			
Employee name	Salary	Job type	Level	Low	Mid	High	Band analysis
Employee 1	$60,000	A	Level 1	$61,600	$75,900	$87,100	Below Range
Employee 2	$81,000	A	Level 1	$61,600	$75,900	$87,000	In Range
Employee 3	$110,000	A	Level 4	$110,000	$115,000	$135,000	In Range
Employee 4	$112,000	A	Level 3	$92,300	$112,300	$128,000	In Range
Employee 5	$60,000	A	Level 2	$49,000	$66,200	$81,400	In Range
Employee 6	$74,000	A	Level 2	$49,000	$66,200	$81,400	In Range
Employee 7	$74,000	A	Level 2	$49,000	$66,200	$81,400	In Range
Employee 8	$104,000	A	Level 2	$74,100	$92,600	$115,000	In Range
Employee 9	$58,000	A	Level 1	$40,400	$49,200	$61,000	In Range

This allows for a more detailed view. I have used employee-level data when with clients to review outliers and summarize total cost to fix below range employees.

This example shows how data graphics are used in human resources consulting. Having the skills to support decision making in your organization through clear information presentations can give you a leg up. Understanding data and making it clear for others through data graphics is the process of becoming visual.

1.4 How Do You Incorporate the Visualization Process Into Practice?

Becoming visual requires many skills. You need to know how to process and mine data to identify findings, produce presentation quality graphics, and communicate your findings to your target audience.

As visualization designers, we are "melding the skills of computer science, statistics, artistic design, and storytelling."
                                        –KATIE CUKIER, 2010, para 3

Expert Practice

Gregory J. Wawro, a professor of Political Science at Columbia University discussed an example of how data graphics supported his teaching.

At the end of the Fall 2016 semester, I was looking for a visualization to help make an argument about what students should expect in terms of the future course of American politics. Many students were confused–some even distraught–about the results of the 2016 U.S. presidential election. I wanted to show them that the outcome was actually not all that unusual if we look at post-WWII dynamics in public policy preferences and partisan control of the presidency. As a political scientist, part of my job is to find systematic explanations for political phenomena, which has become somewhat more difficult given the unusual twists and turns we have witnessed in American politics recently. One thing that I emphasize to students is that political outcomes are often driven by larger, longer term forces that are difficult for individuals or single events to alter. For the 2016 election, a case can be made that the forces in play favored Republicans winning the White House, despite what just about every poll was predicting.

One such force is cyclicity in public opinion with respect to demand for liberal versus conservative policies. James A. Stimson, in his book *Public Opinion in America: Moods, Cycles, and Swings*, developed the concept of "policy mood" to better understand how demand for public policy works. Policy mood refers to "shared feelings" about issues and policies "that move over time and circumstance" and assumes that publics view issues through general dispositions (p. 20). To measure policy mood, Stimson developed a sophisticated algorithm to produce a general measure that aggregates a broad array of items across numerous surveys concerning opinions about various policies and issues. The algorithm addresses difficult problems with survey data, such as missing cases and variations in question wording, to construct a relatively simple, longitudinal measure that indicates whether the polity prefers more liberal or more conservative policies in a given year.

To visualize movement in public opinion and how it relates to election outcomes and representation, I used the ggplot package for R to plot policy mood against a background indicating which party controlled the presidency (higher values for mood indicate a preference for more liberal policies, lower values indicate a preference for more conservative policies).

There are two striking patterns that appear in the plot. The first is that elections tend to produce outcomes that are consistent with the direction of policy mood. When the public wants more conservative policies, the Republicans usually win the White House. When it wants more liberal policies, the Democrats are usually victorious. The second pattern, however, indicates that once a party wins the presidency, mood shifts in the opposite direction of the kind of policies we would anticipate that party to pursue. When Republicans control the White House, which suggests they are moving policy in a more conservative direction, policy mood generally trends in a more liberal direction. When a Democrat is president, policy mood trends in a more conservative direction. For example, mood moved from 59.5 in the first year of the George W. Bush administration to 66.6 during his last year in

Policy Mood and Partisan Control of the Presidency

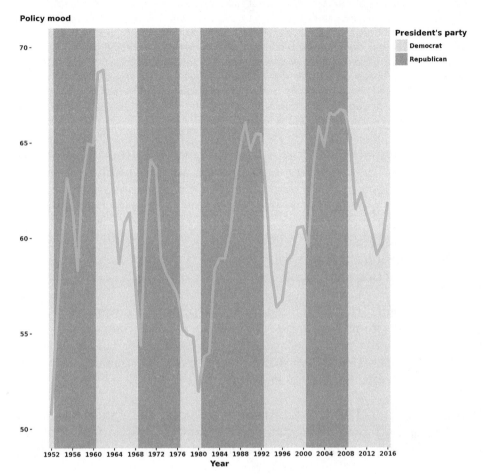

Policy mood

President's party
- Democrat
- Republican

70 -

65 -

60 -

55 -

50 -

1952 1956 1960 1964 1968 1972 1976 1980 1984 1988 1992 1996 2000 2004 2008 2012 2016
Year

office—approximately a 7-point change. During Barack Obama's first year as president, mood was 65.2, but declined to 61.9 at the end of his presidency. Interestingly, in 2015, mood had returned to approximately where it was at the beginning of the Bush administration. This implies that when policy action moves in a particular ideological direction, the public wants it to go in the other direction (or at least wants it to go less in the direction that it is heading). What is somewhat ironic is that, once the party that policy mood indicates is preferred wins the presidency, mood tends to shift away from the ideological predisposition of that party. Perhaps it is the case that the public experiences a kind of "buyers' remorse" when they give a party control of the White House. Or perhaps the party in power enacts policy that goes farther ideologically than what the public wants. Whatever the mechanism behind the pattern, there appears to be a cyclicity to policy mood that is related to oscillating control of the presidency.

Given that policy mood trended significantly in the conservative direction after the election of Obama in 2008, it would not have been surprising to see a Republican elected in 2016, irrespective of who that candidate was. Mood did tick upward just prior to the election, perhaps due to Republicans gaining control of the U.S. Senate after the 2014 elections. Indeed, some of the movement in mood throughout the series seems to be associated with which party controls Congress. In any case, we would predict, based on the historical dynamics revealed in the plot, that mood will trend in the more liberal direction during the presidency of Donald Trump, and if it trends strongly enough in that direction, it may very well lead to Democrats taking back the White House in the 2020 elections.

This example shows how a data graphic was used in classroom teaching to visualize movement in public opinion and how it relates to election outcomes. Throughout the book, practitioners share their practice with you through interviews. Five in-depth use cases with professionals that show you how data graphics are used in the context of work and research.

The followings chapters will guide you in the process of visualizing data for your practice.

CHAPTER II–**THE TOOLS** describes the popular software, platforms, and programming languages used to visualize data.

CHAPTER III–**THE GRAPHICS** presents over 30 types of charts and the insights that they best portray.

CHAPTER IV–**THE DATA** provides techniques for data preparation including data formatting and cleaning. Visual data exploration methods that aid in data understanding are presented with examples.

CHAPTER V–**THE DESIGN** demonstrates the application of design standards to improve readability, clarity, and accessibility of the data insights through graphics.

CHAPTER VI–**THE AUDIENCE** offers practical tips for telling stories with data that will resonate with your audience.

CHAPTER VII–**THE PRESENTATION** offers tactics for designing and delivering data presentations. The common pitfalls and how to avoid them are explained.

CHAPTER VIII–**THE CASES** illustrates how data graphics are used in practice through five case studies. Each case study showcases a unique approach to using data graphics in different settings.

CHAPTER IX–**THE END** synthesizes the key takeaways from each chapter into a concise roadmap to guide your visualization practice.

1.5 Exercises

1. Describe three ways visualization will be used in your workflow and practice.
2. The late Hans Rosling popularized the use of information graphics in presentations. He was a professor of international health and director of the Gapminder Foundation. Using a tool called Trenda-lyzer, Rosling runs an animation that shows the changes in poverty by country. Look at this video and answer the following questions: http://becomingvisual.com/portfolio/hansrosling
    a. Which attributes of Hans Rosling's presentation are especially effective? Explain why.
    b. What questions are being addressed by the presentation?
    c. What data is used to create the visualization?
    d. What symbols are used to represent the data?
3. Build three basic charts (using any visualization tool).
    a. Audience: design a chart for an executive to access sales over the past day.
    b. Data: download the data from http://becomingvisual.com/sales.xls
    c. Insight: show age and gender demographic that has the most sales.
    d. Display: select a chart type that best shows your insight.

Notes

1 The data is from NYC OpenData's website: https://data.cityofnewyork.us
2 "A Census Block Group is a geographical unit used by the United States Census Bureau which is between the Census Tract and the Census Block. It is the smallest geographical unit for which the bureau publishes sample data, i.e. data which is only collected from a fraction of all households" (Wikipedia, 2017, para 1–https://en.wikipedia.org/wiki/Census_block_group). Learn more at: www.census.gov/geo/reference/gtc/gtc_bg.html?cssp=SERP

Icons

Analytics by Kamal from the Noun Project
Big data by Eliricon from the Noun Project
Communication by ProSymbols from the Noun Project

Bibliography

Anscombe, F. J. (1973). Graphs in statistical analysis. *The American Statistician, 27*(1), 17–21. Retrieved from www.sjsu.edu/faculty/gerstman/StatPrimer/anscombe1973.pdf

Christianson, S. (2012). *100 diagrams that changed the world*. New York, NY: Plume.

The City of New York. (2017). 2016 green taxi trip data. Retrieved from https://data.cityofnewyork.us/Transportation/2016-Green-Taxi-Trip-Data/hvrh-b6nb

Cukier, K. (2010). Show me: New ways of visualizing data. Retrieved from www.economist.com/node/15557455

Difference between habit and instinct. (2017). Retrieved from www.differencebetween.info/difference-between-habit-and-instinct

Evelson, B. (2011). What is ADV and why do we need it? Retrieved from http://blogs.forrester.com/boris_evelson/11-11-18-what_is_adv_and_why_do_we_need_it

Evelson, B. (2015). Build more effective data visualizations. Retrieved from http://blogs.forrester.com/boris_evelson/15-10-28-build_more_effective_data_visualizations

The four V's of big data. (2013). Retrieved from www.ibmbigdatahub.com/infographic/four-vs-big-data

Fry, B. (2008). *Visualizing data*. Beijing, China: O'Reilly Media.

Gapminder. Retrieved from www.gapminder.org/

Google trends. Retrieved from https://trends.google.com/trends/

Heer, J., Bostock, M., & Ogievetsky, V. (2010, May 1). A tour through the visualization zoo. *Queue, 8*, 20–30. doi:10.1145/1794514.1805128

NYC wi-fi hotspot locations map. (2017). Retrieved from https://data.cityofnewyork.us/City-Government/NYC-Wi-Fi-Hotspot-Locations-Map/7agf-bcsq

NYPD motor vehicle collisions. (2017). Retrieved from https://data.cityofnewyork.us/Public-Safety/NYPD-Motor-Vehicle-Collisions/h9gi-nx95

Playfair, W. (1786). *Commercial and political atlas* (1st ed.). Printed for J. Debrett, London. (3rd ed., 1801) Printed for J. Wallis, London.

Rosling, H. (2006). The best stats you've ever seen. Retrieved from www.ted.com/talks/hans_rosling_shows_the_best_stats_you_ve_ever_seen

Ware, C. (2008). *Visual thinking for design*. Burlington, MA: Morgan Kaufmann

Wong, D. M. (2010). *The Wall Street Journal guide to information graphics: The dos and don'ts of presenting data, facts, and figures*. New York, NY: W. W. Norton & Company.

Yau, N. (2011). *Visualize this: The FlowingData guide to design, visualization, and statistics*. Indianapolis, IN: Wiley.

Yau, N. (2013). *Data points: Visualization that means something*. Indianapolis, IN: Wiley.

II

THE
TOOLS

Which software should you use to build data graphics?

To incorporate visualization into your practice, you must know which tools are best suited for the visualization task. The tools available for building visualizations fall into four categories: 1) basic productivity applications, 2) visualization software, 3) business intelligence tools, and 4) developer-based packages. Getting started with each is very straightforward. The difficulty comes in identifying what you want to visualize and ensuring your data is in the correct format. This chapter presents the options for creating data graphics and criteria for evaluating your software choices.

2.1 Basic Productivity Applications

Common productivity tools are good enough for most visualization tasks. With Excel or the iWork suite, you can create basic chart types: bar, pie, line, and scatter plots in addition to more sophisticated displays such as stacked area and radar charts. Google Charts are also interactive and web-based.

MICROSOFT EXCEL

Microsoft Excel provides a sophisticated set of static charting options. These include column and horizontal bars, line, pie, area, radar, scatterplot, and spark lines. Excel is designed for working with data. Excel supports the pre-processing data and visualization in the same application. Charts created in Excel are easily ported to PowerPoint and Word. Excel charts require customization to adhere to many of the design standards presented in this book. For instance, the default charts contain unnecessary non-data elements such as gridlines, tick marks, and borders.

If you use Excel exclusively in your practice, consider creating chart templates to which you can apply your own chart style. http://becomingvisual.com/portfolio/excel

See Figure 2.1 for an example of a radar chart created in Microsoft Excel.

The number of bicycle rentals reaches highs in July but lows in August and September during hurricane season

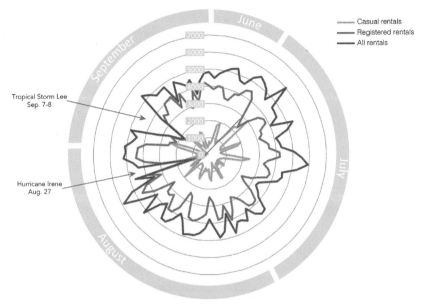

Nicole Bohorad | Source: Fanaee-T, H. & Gama, J. (2013)

Figure 2.1 A radar chart created in Microsoft Excel

 Managers may do their analyses in Excel but present their charts in PowerPoint. There are additional plug-ins, for PowerPoint that extend the chart features and options. These include charting, layout, and additional data formatting features. Learn more at: http://becomingvisual.com/portfolio/powerpoint.

iWORK

Apple's own productivity suite, iWork, which includes Pages, Numbers, and Keynote, offers basic 2D and 3D charts in addition to animated vertical and horizontal bars, scatter plots, and bubble charts.

As with Excel, the default charts in iWork require that you reformat the default features to conform to your own aesthetic. The color templates provided simplify the process of removing non-data elements that may interfere with interpretation of the data.

See Figure 2.2 for an example of a chart created in iWork's Pages.

The number of three-point shots attempted in the NBA has increased over 1,224% since the three-point shot was introduced.

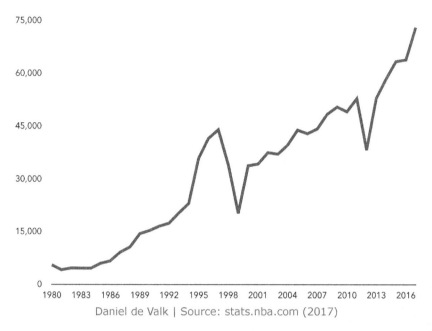

Daniel de Valk | Source: stats.nba.com (2017)

Figure 2.2 A time series chart created in iWork's Pages of the number of three-point shot attempts in the NBA

Users who work with data in Excel can easily import their data to iWork's Numbers, Pages, or Keynote. PC users can use Apple's iWork productivity suite using iWork for iCloud.

GOOGLE CHARTS

Google offers a free and open option for creating a variety of data graphics. The charts integrate seamlessly with the Google Apps suite (Docs, Sheets, and Slides). Google Charts offers more options than Excel or iWork including interactive, animated, and geospatial data graphics. For more robust reporting and visualization tools in one, see Google's Data Studio.

For a gallery of chart possibilities, go to: http://becomingvisual.com/portfolio/googlecharts

The world's top container shipping ports
(in millions of TEUs)

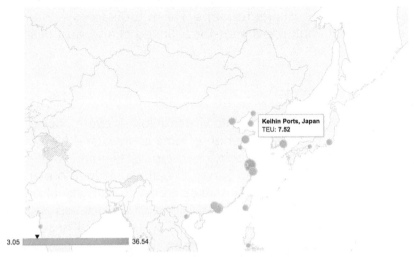

Kristen Sosulski | Logistics Management (2017)

Figure 2.3 A GeoChart with bubble markers created in Google Charts

See Figure 2.3 for an example of a GeoChart (point map) created in Google Charts. The chart shows the locations of the world's top container shipping ports, measured in millions of TEUs (20-foot equivalent units).

Microsoft Excel, iWork, and Google Charts all enable you to create static charts. Interactive web-based charts can be created using Google Charts. These charts require coding in JavaScript and knowledge of HTML. Use basic productivity tools when working with single tables of data in. csv format or. xlsx. When files sizes approach a gigabyte, they become unmanageable using these tools. Large data sets are typically hosted externally, in the cloud, and queried using specialized business intelligence tools and programming platforms.

 Follow the tutorial in Exercise 1 on page xx to create the chart above.

2.2 Visualization Software

Data visualization software applications are ubiquitous. These applications focus on usability through a drag and drop interface. They are designed for everyone from novices to expert visualization designers and analysts. Tableau Desktop and many other specialized data visualization software packages (e.g., QlikView, Domo) offer an interface for visualizing data. These applications offer a full-range of data graphics from basic charts to maps. These tools feature Interactive, static, animated, multiple-dimensional linked charts, and dashboard displays.

TABLEAU DESKTOP

Tableau is one of the leading data visualization software packages. It is designed to integrate with a range of data sources and file types. For example, you can import the basic. xls,. cvs, or. txt files and connect them to live data sources on Tableau Server, Oracle, Amazon, Cloudera, etc.

The drag and drop interface makes it easy to start visualizing your variables. The design of the charts and tables produced in Tableau are inspired by the *Grammar of Graphics* by Leland Wilkinson. Therefore, the graphics need little refinement in terms of the 10 design standards discussed in Chapter V–THE DESIGN. Interactive, spatial, animated, linked, and dashboard displays are all possible with Tableau Desktop.

Tableau has robust capabilities for filtering, grouping, clustering, aggregating, and disaggregating variables. Some programming knowledge is required for complex analytical tasks. As one would create a formula in Excel, users of Tableau can create new fields and perform mathematical computations.

Tableau workbooks easily publish to the web with Tableau public, a free service. Tableau workbooks can also be shared securely across an organization with Tableau server, an additional service. Figure 2.4 shows an interactive Tableau data graphic with an option to filter by year.

ARCGIS

There are specialized software packages that focus on specific data graphics such as geospatial displays. ArcGIS is a mapping platform available for desktop or online. It is a platform that visualizes and analyzes most types of spatial data. There are many types of ready to use base maps, demographic and lifestyle maps, historical maps, and layers for boundaries and places, landscapes, oceans, earth observations, transportation, and urban systems. ArcGIS offers 3D mapping as well. See Figure 2.5 for an example of a map of shipping container volume by country using ArcGIS online.

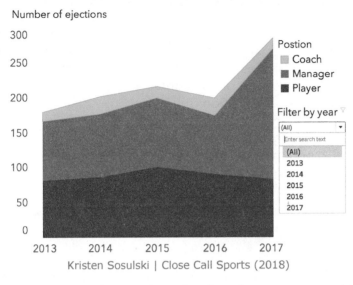

Number of game ejections by position

Number of ejections

Kristen Sosulski | Close Call Sports (2018)

Figure 2.4 An interactive data graphic with a drop-down menu created in Tableau Desktop

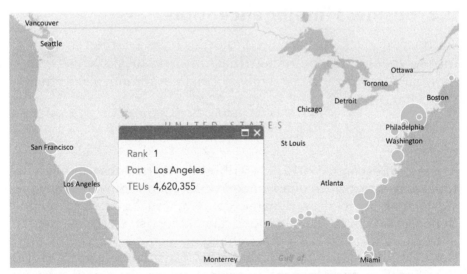

Kristen Sosulski | Logistics Management (2017)

Figure 2.5 A simple bubble map created in ArcGIS of the top 30 shipping ports in the United States by container volume

CURIOUS HOW TO VISUALIZING BIG DATA IN 3D OR USING VIRTUAL REALITY?

QuantumViz is a big data visualization software company that allows data scientists and analysts to find insights in massive datasets and create amazing data stories in 3D, VR, or AR. For example, they helped develop a geo-visualization of container ships movement through the Panama Canal. In addition, their storyboard feature allows users to build a data-story that includes 360 images and videos, such as a 360 image showing a cargo shipping passing through a gate. All of this can be experienced in VR as well. QuantumViz's revolutionary tool transforms data visualizations into data experiences.

Learn more: http://becomingvisual.com/portfolio/quantumviz

The level of design and analytical sophistication with software like Tableau and ArcGIS is much higher than the basic productivity tools such as those offered by Excel.

2.3 Business Intelligence Tools

At the next level, modern technologies have enabled the use of more dynamic and interactive business graphics, such as real-time dashboards and charts that update automatically as the data changes.

(FORRESTER RESEARCH, 2012, p. 4)

Forrester Research (2012) describes these business intelligence tools as the next wave of advanced visualization software. They provide the ability to show dynamic content, visual querying, multiple dimensional-linked visualizations, animated visualizations, personalization, and alerts based on changing data. Examples of these business intelligence tools include IBM Watson Analytics, SAS, TIBCO's SpotFire, and Microsoft's Power BI. All require a paid subscription or license. Each provides an interface for data querying and exploration. Most of these tools offer visualization recommendations as well.

IBM WATSON ANALYTICS

Watson Analytics provides a platform for users to explore their data, ask questions of their data, and create data graphics. Watson is unique in that it guides the user in selecting the best method of inquiry to learn about the data. A set of exploratory visualizations called spirals are presented (see Figure 2.6). The spirals show the drivers of the target variable, for example, what factors contribute to the total dollar amount spent by a customer in a casino? The user can then build data graphics with recommendations from Watson.

2.4 Programming Packages

For developers, analysts, and designers who want to visualize data in their own programming environment, there are several contenders. Most programming languages have data graphic packages. Python and R have a sophisticated set of libraries or packages for data visualization. In addition, there are numerous JavaScript libraries for web-based data graphics.

R AND RSTUDIO

R is a free open-source statistical programming language. There are several packages that are used for visualization in R.
These include:

- graphics
- ggplot2
- car
- lattice
- ndtv
- ggvis
- plotly
- shiny

R is capable of both data analysis and data graphics. However, the default chart output requires refinements to aesthetic elements (such as colors). For example, look at Figure 2.7. This plot lacks a title. The gray background and gridlines do not add any information to the display. The black dots are harsh. They can be changed to a lighter color

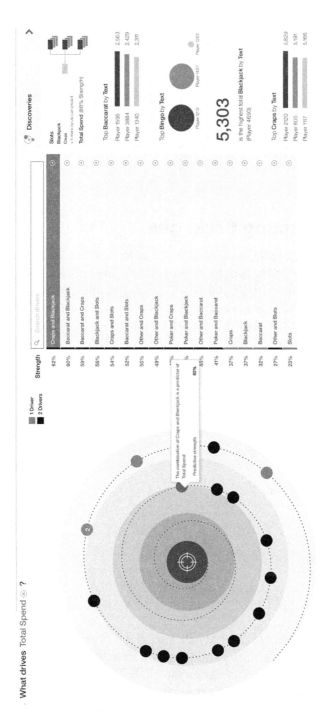

Figure 2.6 The spiral visualizations generated from Watson that shows the predictive strength of a given variable (denoted by gray and black bubbles) to the target variable (the center of the spiral)

Bicycle rentals are positively associated with warmer temperatures.

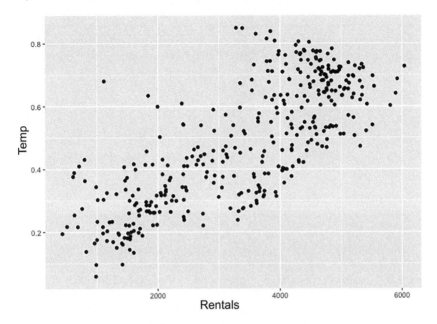

Figure 2.7 A default scatterplot produced by the ggplot2 package in R

once the background is removed. Also, notice how the x-axis begins at 2000 and the scale for temperature is undefined. Fortunately, the plot can be revised as shown in Figure 2.8. Note the x and y scales, the labeling of axes, title, data source, and simple white background with green points.

The ggthemes package can be used to customize the non-data elements of graphs produced in ggplot2. The bw() theme was applied to Figure 2.8 for a simple black and white color scheme. The point color was changed from black to green.

The **ggvis** package in R produces graphs that apply many more of the accepted data visualization design principles. It leverages some of the interactive components of the **shiny** package for interactive web applications. Shiny applications can be published to the web and include animated or interactive visualizations. R's geomapping capabilities are somewhat limited in comparison with ArcGIS.

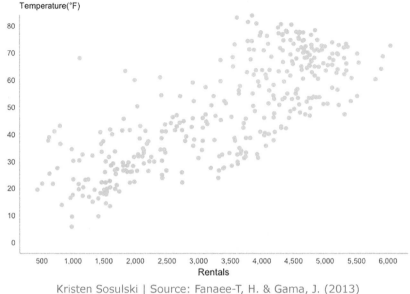

Kristen Sosulski | Source: Fanaee-T, H. & Gama, J. (2013)

Figure 2.8 A customized scatterplot produced by the ggplot2 package in R

PYTHON

Python is a powerful programming language with stellar data cleaning and data manipulation capabilities. Python's **matplotlib** package is used to plot basic charts. Packages such as Seaborn yield high-quality data graphics.

Some of Python's other data visualization libraries include:

- geoplotlib
- Bokeh
- Pandas
- Altair
- ggplot
- pygal
- plotly

JAVASCRIPT

JavaScript is a web-based scripting language that is used in combination with HTML.

Some JavaScript libraries include D3, rCharts, HighCharts, charts.js, dimple.js, and processing.js. These libraries allow users to create

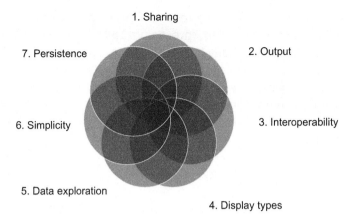

1. Sharing
7. Persistence
2. Output
6. Simplicity
3. Interoperability
5. Data exploration
4. Display types

Figure 2.9 Criteria for evaluating software for visualizing data

highly sophisticated web-based visualizations. The libraries are freely available and interact with plotly as the platform for displaying the charts and graphs. The learning curve is very steep. Skills in working with HTML and JSON data are required.

Check out more options for data visualization JavaScript libraries: http://becomingvisual.com/portfolio/javascript

2.5 A Criteria for Selecting Tools to Build Data Graphics

A SOFTWARE EVALUATION CHECKLIST FOR DATA GRAPHICS

When evaluating a new data visualization tool, consider the following (aside from price):

☐ Sharing: can others view and edit your visualization and analysis? The ability to share your charts and graphs with others promotes collaboration on data visualization tasks.

☐ Output: can you publish visualizations to the web, create high-quality print graphics, and embed them in other applications? The ultimate destination of your visualization will dictate your tool choice. For example, if your audience is viewing your graphs online, you may want to make them interactive to facilitate exploration.

☐ Interoperability: how easily can you connect to other data sources? For example, does the software allow you to import diverse file types, such as. xlsx,. csv, or. txt, and also link to databases?

☐ Display types: what types of visualizations do you need to build? Maps, networks, and text-based visualizations are not available in every tool.

☐ Data exploration: do you need a tool to explore your data and present it visually? Features such as visual querying are not standard in every tool.

☐ Simplicity: do you want to create charts and graphs quickly? Some tools require a steep learning curve, even to build a simple bar chart.

☐ Persistence: do you think you'll need to revise the visualizations you create? Choose a tool from a reputable company that you think will be around for a while.

Before using a free data visualization tool, know how your data are stored. A major drawback with most free apps is that they require you to make your data public in exchange for being a freemium member. Consider looking into a premium membership to protect your data.

There is no one-size-fits-all solution to visualizing geospatial, categorical, time series, statistical, and network data as static, animated, or interactive displays for the desktop, web, or a presentation.

Select the tools that work best for your workflow. If you do all of your analysis in Excel, consider learning the nuances of the chart options for the basic chart types, such as bar, pie, and line charts. Then, explore other tools, such as Tableau, to easily create maps, interactive data graphics, and animated charts.

Interview With a Practitioner

I interviewed Christian from Viant, who described how he uses data graphics to support his work.

 Kristen Sosulski (KS)   **Christian Theodore (CT)**

KS:

Who are you and what do you do?

CT:

My name is Christian Theodore. I work as a data analyst on the Attribution Platform Team for Viant Inc.

KS:

How do you use data visualization in your practice?

CT:

I use data visualization to help end users move from the complex to the simple. My primary function is to build innovative client-facing products at Viant while applying the principles of data visualization. At Viant, we offer a suite of solutions to help our clients: 1) understand their audience segments, 2) gains insights on the performance of their digital marketing campaigns, and ultimately 3) use those insights towards better decision making.

MTA LAST TOUCH TO CONVERSION

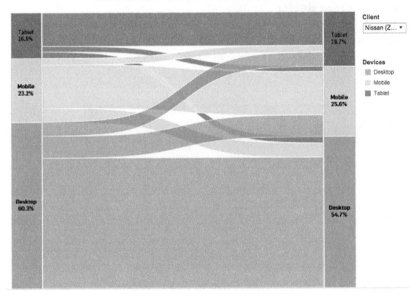

As a recent example of how I apply data visualization to my practice, I used a Sankey Diagram to illustrate how different devices drive conversions after users see a client's ad. The core idea was to illustrate how impressions across multiple devices can be attributed to a user's conversion (a "conversion" can be defined as the user taking whatever specified call to action the marketer intended, via the ad).

The chart is composed of three main elements (from left to right):

1.   The Source Stacked Bar Chart
2.   The Flow Ribbons
3.   The Destination Stacked Bar Chart

In detail, here is what each element represents:

1.   A "source" bar chart, which displays the proportion of last-touch (that is, immediately prior to conversion) ad impressions accounted for by device type.
2.   The "flow ribbons," which show the percentage of conversions attributed by device (see screenshot below). The branches in each ribbon show how the source device differs from the destination device. In the below example, the highlighted strand indicates that **7.9% (34,527) of people who last saw an ad on a desktop computer converted on their mobile phone.** Overall, the volume of conversions (indicated by the thickness of each strand) shows that the majority of people convert on the same device on which they last saw an ad**, but a significant minority convert on a different device**.
3.   The "destination" bar chart gives an aggregate picture of the overall distribution of conversions by device.

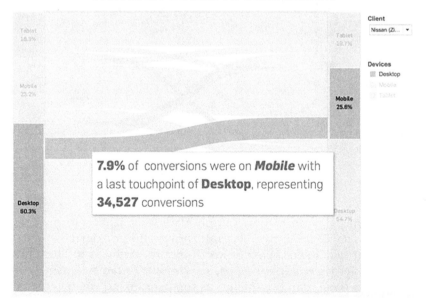

MTA LAST TOUCH TO CONVERSION

7.9% of conversions were on **Mobile** with a last touchpoint of **Desktop**, representing **34,527** conversions

KS:

What insights are evidenced by the graph provided?

CT:

The chart delivers several powerful insights:

1. It illustrates the direct pathway users follow from the last touchpoint to conversion. This is valuable for advertisers, as it helps to answer the question:
    Do Customers Typically Convert on the Same Device on Which They Last Saw the ad?
2. It allows advertisers to make more informed decisions about their budgeting strategies. In cases where ad spend is skewed to a particular device, the chart helps to validate that strategy is best, or can suggest that the advertiser change its strategy, based on the devices where conversions occur For example, a desktop may drive the majority of conversions, but a mobile device may still provide value, and therefore not be discounted as merely a touchpoint (that is, **investment in mobile is still a good strategy**).

KS:

How did you create it? What was the data? What was the software? What would have been the alternative?

CT:

This chart was created using Tableau Desktop, leveraging its built-in Data Densification feature, creating Padded Bins, and finally, incorporating a mathematical function to trace the path of each conversion.
The data was obtained from a sample of data culled from a few of Viant's MTA (Muti-Touch Attribution) client reports.

This example shows how data graphics are used to show the pathways of conversions for specific Viant clients. These pathways are the visual evidence that inform decisions about which platforms to use to reach Viant's client's target market.

Software is not magic. As evidenced by the Viant case, there is quite a bit of technical detail involved in creating sophisticated data graphics. Use the tools that best suit you and your work environment. Use the checklist presented to guide you in the software selection process. There are many visualization software packages (desktop and cloud-based) available. However, with the cloud-based solutions, there may be data privacy issues. In addition, many software packages are not equipped to handle large data sets.

As a next step, I encourage you to create several charts using basic productivity tools and apply the design standards (see Chapter V–THE DESIGN). You'll begin to see which tools work best for your visualization needs.

2.6 Exercises

1. Recreate the chart in Figure 2.2.
    a. Explore Google's Visualization API at https://developers. google.com/chart/
    b. Select the GeoMap.
    c. Cut and paste the GeoMap code into a text document using a text editor such as NotePad.
    d. Save and name the document with an. html extension.
    e. Drag and drop the. html document into your browser window to see the map.
    f. Go back to the. html document and edit the data to reflect the top 5 shipping ports instead of the default data provided. The shipping port data can be found at: http://becomingvisual/ portfolio/shipping
2. Create a simple bar chart with the same data used in exercise 1 using both Excel and Tableau Desktop. Compare and contrast the amount of effort required and the quality of the output.
3. Practice building basic charts and maps. I've created three simple tutorials to follow for creating a bar chart, table, and point map in Tableau. Try to customize the chart to make it look like the example provided.
    a. Bar chart tutorial: http://becomingvisual.com/portfolio/bar-graph
    b. Table tutorial: http://becomingvisual.com/portfolio/table-graph
    c. Point map tutorial: http://becomingvisual.com/portfolio/point-map

Bibliography

Evelson, B., & Yuhanna, N. (2002). The Forrester Wave: Advanced Data Visualization (ADV) Platforms, Q3 2012.

III
THE
GRAPHICS

Which chart works best to show my data and insight?

Selecting the right visualization to present your data is complicated: the number of chart choices can distract you from the goal of communicating the key insight. This chapter reveals how the insight and data drive your selection of the right chart.

Each type of chart is designed to show a type of data in a particular way. For example:

- Horizontal bar charts show rank well by ordering bars from largest to smallest.
- Line charts convey a change over a specified period of time, such as the unemployment rate per month over a 12-month period.
- Point maps effectively demarcate precise locations, such as the address of each public school in a district.
- Filled or choropleth maps allow for the comparison of regions, such as the GDP of each African country. Each region is filled with a shade. The darker the shade the higher the value.

Two maps are presented in Figure 3.1. Chart A is a filled map showing the locations of recycling bins in NYC by an aggregated measure (zip code). Chart B shows the actual location of each recycling bin.

Which map communicates the data best?

The short answer is: it depends. Do you want to show the aggregated total number of recycling bins per neighborhood as shown in Chart A? Or would you rather show the concentration of the location of individual recycling bins within neighborhoods as shown in Chart B? As a data graphic designer, you decide.

The data graphics choices presented in this chapter will point you in the right direction based on your data. The type of chart you ultimately select is limited by the type of data. Data comes in many forms. Forms include categorical, univariate (a single variable), multivariate (more than one variable), geospatial, time series, network, or text. Certain charts display comparisons, distributions, proportions, relationships, locations, trends, connections, or sentiment better than others. Refer to Table 3.1 for guidance on the types of insights you can visualize based on your data.

This table should serve as a handy reference throughout the book.

Selecting the right chart
There are many available resources to guide you in determining the right chart for your data. Learn more at: http://becomingvisual.com/portfolio/chartpickers

Chart A: Recycling bins grouped by zip code

Number of bins

1   21

Chart B: Recycling bins grouped by individual locations

Kristen Sosulski | Source: NYC Open Data (2014)

Figure 3.1 Chart A and Chart B use the same data two different ways.

Table 3.1 The general data insight that corresponds to each data classification

Data	Example	Insight	Chart type
Categorical	Non-numeric data such as types of movies, books, or authors.	Comparisons, proportions	Vertical bar, column bar, horizontal bar, and bullet charts Pie, stacked bar, stacked 100% bar, stacked area, stacked 100% area, and a tree map
Univariate	One numeric variable, such as book price	Distributions, proportions, frequencies	Histogram, density plot, and a boxplot
Geospatial	Specific locations marked by the latitude and longitude, regions coded by zip code, city, state, country, or county boundaries	Locations, comparisons, trends	Choropleth filled-map, bubble map, point map, connection map, and isopleth map
Multivariate	Two or more numeric variables, for example, weight, height, and IQ	Relationships, proportions, comparisons	Scatterplot, scatterplot matrix, bubble, parallel coordinates, radar, bullet, and a heat map.
Time series	Years, months, days, hours, minutes, seconds, or date	Trends, comparisons, cycles	Line chart, sparkline, area, stream graph, as well as bubble, stacked-area, and vertical bar charts.
Text	Single words or phrases, such as keywords from restaurant reviews on Yelp	Sentiment, comparisons, frequency	Word cloud, proportional area chart using size bubbles or squares, histogram, and bar chart
Edge lists or adjacency matrices	Who contacts whom or who knows whom in a network	Connections, relationships, tie strength, centrality, interactions	Undirected network diagram and directed network diagram

3.1 Comparisons of Categories and Time

Table 3.2 presents charts that compare values or quantities either over time or to each other.

Questions:

1. What's the best? What's the worst? Compared to what?
2. Who's ranked the highest? The lowest?
3. How does performance compare to the target or goal? For example, did total sales exceed the forecast?

Insight: use comparisons to illustrate the similarities and differences among categories. This includes the minimum value, maximum value, rank, performance, sum, totals, counts, and quantities.

Data: aggregated categorical data, such as the number of books sold by author. Time series data can be shown as a categorical variable. For example, each year can be a category.

Chart options: vertical bar, column bar, horizontal bar, and bullet charts.

Table 3.2 Chart types to present categorical data

Chart type	Description and design considerations
Vertical bar	Bars are arranged vertically on the x-axis. Each bar represents a category or sub-category. The bar height measures the quantity (count) or sum. • Keep bars the same color and shade when they measure the same variable (Wong, 2010). • Use a zero baseline for the y-axis. • Show negative values below the baseline. • Keep the width of the bar about twice the width of the space between the bars (Wong, 2010).
Column bar	Column bar charts present two series for each category. • Use different color shading for each series. • Shade bars from lightest to darkest (Wong, 2010).
Horizontal bar	Bars are arranged horizontally, rather than vertically. • Best used for ranking, such as first place, second place, third place. • Arrange bars in descending order, from largest to smallest.
Bullet	Bullet charts display performance of a variable as a horizontal bar compared to a target or goal, represented by a vertical line. For example, a bullet chart could show whether the actual sales for a given period(s) are above/ below target sales. The performance measure (horizontal bar) overlays several shaded rectangles that represent qualitative ranges (e.g., 40% to the target goal, to indicate the performance progress).

3.2 Distributions

Table 3.3 presents options for showing possible values (or intervals) of the data and how often they occur. These types of charts can reveal the minimum and maximum values, median, outliers, median, frequency, and probability densities.

Questions:

1. What are the highest, middle, and lowest values?
2. Does one thing stand out from the rest?
3. What does the shape of the data look like?

Insight: use to distributions charts reveal outliers, the shape of the distribution, frequencies, range of values, minimum value, maximum value, and the median.
Data: univariate or a single numeric variable.
Chart options: histogram, density plot, and a boxplot.

Table 3.3 Chart types for showing distributions

Chart type	Description and design considerations
Histogram	Histograms show frequencies of a single variable grouped into bins or frequency ranges on the x-axis. The y-axis of the histogram shows the frequency count or percentage. • A large bin size can obscure the data. • Adjust the size of the bins to best reveal the shape of the frequency distribution.
Density plot	Density plots show probability densities and the distribution of a single variable. The area under the curve emphasizes the shape of the distribution of data. Annotate the mean to draw attention to the center of the distribution.
Boxplot	Boxplots show the range of a single variable including the minimum, 25th percentile, 50th percentile, median (not the average), 75th percentile, and the maximum value. Boxplots are helpful to spot outliers.

3.3 Proportions

Table 3.4 presents options for displaying individual parts of a whole. This enables comparisons among subcategories by evaluating relative proportions, for example, demographics by neighborhood.

Questions:

1. What are the parts that make up the whole?
2. What part is the largest or smallest?
3. What parts are similar or dissimilar?

Insight: use to show summaries, similarities, anomalies, percentage related to the whole (by category, subcategory, and over time).
Data: single categorical variable with subcategories, two or more variables. A time dimension can also be included.
Chart options: pie, stacked bar, stacked 100% bar, stacked area, stacked 100% area, tree map, and doughnut chart.

3.4 Relationships

Table 3.5 presents options for displaying multivariate data. These charts show how one or more variables relates to other variables. For example, how do sales affect profitability by region?

Questions:

1. Is the relationship positive, negative, or neither?
2. How are x and y related to each other?
3. What makes one group or cluster different from another?

Insight: use to show outliers, correlations, positive, and negative relationships among two or more variables.
Data: two or more numeric variables.
Chart options: scatterplot, scatterplot matrix, bubble, parallel coordinates, radar, bullet, and a heat map.

3.5 Locations

Geospatial visualizations require data that corresponds to geography (e.g., latitude and longitude). Table 3.6 presents the options for showing these location types. These geospatial displays can identify places, population differences, concentrations, and distances.

Table 3.4 Chart options for showing proportions

Chart type	Description and design considerations
Pie 	Pie charts show proportions within a whole. The slices are subcategories of a single category. Slices add up to 100% or 1. • Avoid using pie charts if all the slices are similar in size. • Limit pie charts to eight slices or less (Wong, 2010). • Label directly on the pie slices, rather than using a legend. • Keep pie slices the same color. Use the whitespace between slices to differentiate the slices.
Stacked bar 	Stacked bar charts show proportions and quantities within a whole category. They show absolute and relative differences. • Limit the number of subcategories to four or less. • Use stacked bars that add up to 100% to show the relative differences between quantities within each group.
Stacked area 	Stacked area charts highlight the absolute and relative differences between two or more series. They are line charts with the area below the line filled in with color. To show relative differences use a 100% stacked area chart. Label each series directly, if possible over using a legend.
Tree map 	Tree maps show parts of the whole by using nested rectangles. Each rectangle is designated a size and a shade of a color. This enables you to emphasize both the importance (usually shown by size) and urgency (usually represented by color) of a data point. • Used often for portfolio analysis to highlight similarities and anomalies. • Usually require interactivity such as mouse-over, to read the subcategory labels for the smallest rectangles. • This chart type is best used for analysis and exploration rather than presentation.
Doughnut 	Doughnut charts present proportions of a whole through slices of a doughnut shaped graphic It is just a pie chart with the center missing. This type of chart can contain multiple series, represented as doughnuts arranged inside one another.

Table 3.5 Chart options for showing relationships between two or more variables

Chart type	Description and design considerations
Scatterplot	Scatterplots show relationships between two variables. For example, they show the change in x given y. • Use to show positive or negative correlations, or linear and nonlinear relationships between variables. • Labeling of every data point reduces readability but increases interpretation.
Scatterplot matrix	Scatterplot matrices help identify a correlation between multiple variables. It makes it easy to observe the relationship between pairs of variables in one set of plots. This chart type is best reserved for exploration versus presentation.
Bubble chart	A bubble chart is a scatterplot that shows relationships between three or four variables. The position of the bubble shows the relationship between the x and y variables. • The bubble size is based upon a numerical variable, such as population, or sales. • The bubble color is best reserved for categorical data, such as region. • Bubble charts are best when the bubble sizes vary significantly.
Parallel coordinates	Parallel coordinates map each column in a data table as a vertical parallel line with its own axis. Each observation (row) is represented by a point on the parallel line. That point is then connected to the next point on the next parallel line by a horizontal line. • Use the technique of highlighting the lines that touch any number of values in either of the categories, called brushing, to provide data context while focusing on select series. • This chart type is best reserved for exploration over presentation.

Table 3.5 (Continued)

Chart type	Description and design considerations
Radar 	Radar charts compare multiple numerical variables. They show which variables have similar values, and to spot outliers, high values, and low values. Each variable is provided its own individual axis, but the axes are arranged radially. Every observation connects to form a shaded polygon. • Limit the number of variables to reduce the number of axes to increase readability. • Scaling is affected when variables have dissimilar minimum and maximum ranges.
Heat map 	A heat map is a graphical representation of a table of data. The individual values are arranged in a table/matrix and represented by colors. Use grayscale or gradient for coloring. Sorting of the variables changes the color pattern.
Small multiples	A series of similar graphs that use the same scale. This allows for easy comparisons between variables. A single chart represents each categorical variable, such as sales personnel; the individual charts are grouped together on a single display. • Allows easy comparisons by using the same scale for each chart • Avoid showing too much detail in any individual chart.

Questions:

1. Where can the most or least be found?
2. How does one area compare to another?
3. What is the distance from one place to another?
4. How does a variable change by location?

Insight: use to demonstrate similarities and differences by location, density, distance, and counts (such as population).

Data: latitude and longitude, zip codes, census tracks, cities, states, countries, and regions.

Table 3.6 Chart options for showing locations

Chart type	Description and design considerations
Choropleth or filled maps	Choropleth maps fill regions with color. A color gradient and density distinguishes regions from one another. Use to compare different regions such as continents, countries, states, territories, zip codes, or census tracks.
	Provide a legend. Keep the gradient of colors within a limited range. This will allow the reader to easily compare the regions.
Point map	Point maps show a specific location. These dots can vary in size, form, or color.
	Point maps illustrate density when the individual locations are easily distinguishable. Too many points can obscure the location. Consider the size of the points and the labeling of the points.
Symbol or bubble map	Symbol maps are point maps that use different sized bubbles or shapes to mark a location. These symbols are sized by a certain variable.
	Too many or too large bubbles can obscure the locations referenced.
Connection or path maps	Connection maps graph a line from one or more points to another. Use to show distances or pathways between one or more locations.
	Use high contrasting colors for the map projection and the lines that connect the points. Avoid too many overlapping lines.
Geographic heat map (Isopleth)	Isopleth maps show gradual change over geography. This technique uses a color value (lightness/darkness) and hue to show density. The color value is not constrained by boundary lines (e.g., such as zip code).
	Use for events that are continuous and unbounded (e.g., such as temperature).

Chart options: use a choropleth-filled map for comparing regions; bubble or point maps to mark a location while showing quantities or categories; connection maps to show distances; and isopleth maps to show variables, such as temperature, that are unrestrained by boundaries (e.g., city, state, zip code).

About geocoding
Geocoding is the process of transforming a description of a location, such as an address, to a location on the Earth's surface. This will take the form of numerical coordinates such as latitude and longitude. Reverse geocoding is the process of converting numerical coordinates into a description of that location. Learn more at: http://becomingvisual.com/portfolio/geocode

About Map Projections
Geographical data is plotted on a map projection. The most common are Albers and Mercator. Select the most appropriate map projection for your data. Use the Mercator projection to preserve angles and shapes in small areas. The Mercator projection is also good for presenting connection maps that show routes and paths for directions. The standard Albers projection can be used to present U.S. census or government data. This equal-rectangular projection is a good option for thematic world mappings. Learn more at: http://becomingvisual.com/portfolio/mapprojections

3.6 Trends–Showing Comparisons Over Time or Composition Over Time

Table 3.7 presents several charts to show how one or more variables changes over time; for example, the growth of Internet usage by country over time or number of Twitter posts per minute over a 24-hour period. Relationships, locations, proportions, comparisons, and distributions can have a time dimension.

Questions:

- What changed today from yesterday?
- How does time of year affect sales, results, outcomes, etc.?
- What times are the most popular? Least popular?

Insight: change over time, cycles, or comparisons over time.
Data: time dimension such as year, month, day, hour, minute, second, date, quarter, season, century, decade, etc.
Chart options: line chart, sparkline, area, and stream graph. The bubble, stacked-area, and vertical bar charts are options as well.

Table 3.7 Chart options for showing trends

Chart type	Description and design considerations
Line chart	Line charts show the change over time for one or more series (sales per hour). The line connects each data point in the series (shown or not). The y-axis baseline should be equal or less than the minimum value in the data. • Show four or fewer series of lines on a line chart (Wong, 2010). • Label each series directly or use an ordered legend.
Sparkline	A sparkline is a line chart without axes or much detail. It is a small graphic designed to give a quick representation of change over time. • Not intended to provide the quantitative precision of a normal line graph. • Label the last data point to provide additional information.
Area graph	Area graphs are line charts with the area below the line filled in with color. They can show a single series or multiple time series using stacked areas. Use the same color for the line and the area beneath it. See Table 3.4 for use of stacked areas to show proportional change over time.
Stream graph	Stream graphs show changes over time for different data series. Color is used to distinguish the categories. Each stream represents a single category proportional change over time. Stream graphs are used to provide a general overview, not when accuracy is important. Use for large time series data sets with five or fewer categories.

With time series data, beware of interpolation, a method of constructing new data points within the range of a discrete set of known data points. If you do not have many known values, consider plotting each data point without a line; a line chart could lead to incorrect estimated values.

3.7 Word Frequency and Sentiment

Table 3.8 presents options for visualizing textual data (for example, to show how frequently words appear in a given body of text by making the size of each word proportional to its frequency). Frequency of words may include added dimensions categorized by sentiment, such as positivity or negativity of each word.

Questions:

- How many times does a given word or phrase appear?
- What words or phrases appear most often? Least often?
- What words appear together?
- Are most words or phrases positive or negative?

Insight: frequency or counts of words and phrases. The count of the positive or negative direction of the sentiment of the words or phrases.
Data: text as single words, or n-grams (one or more words that appear together in text).
Chart options: word cloud, proportional area chart using size bubbles or squares, and histogram.

Table 3.8 Chart options for showing sentiment and frequency words

Chart type	Description and design considerations
Word cloud	Words are arranged in a cluster or cloud of words. Words can be arranged in any format: horizontal lines, columns, or within a shape.
	Color is used to categorize words by sentiment, or another categorical variable.
Proportional bubble area chart	Words are ranked by their frequency. The frequency is represented by sized bubbles or squares. The bubbles /squares are arranged in a grid with words on the x-axis and observation on y.
	Works well for the top 10 words (difficult to view beyond that).

Learn more about software options for creating word clouds at:
http://becomingvisual.com/portfolio/wordclouds

3.8 Connections and Networks

Table 3.9 shows how connections between people or entities can be represented within a network (such as a school, organization, or structure). For example, a diagram may show who is following whom on Twitter. These are known as social graphs. They show the representation of the interconnection of relationships in an online social network.

In addition, a network diagram can help explain which employees are most critical to certain tasks, how students in a school are grouping, and so on.

Table 3.9 Chart options for showing networks

Chart type	Description and design considerations
Network diagram (undirected)	Undirected network diagrams depict equal relationships between individual entities. Each entity is referred to as a node, represented as a bubble. The relationships between the entities are shown as lines known as edges. The thicker the line, the stronger the relationship. The position of the nodes shows centrality in the network and distance from other nodes. Minimize edge (line) crossing (Ognyanova, K, 2016).
Network diagram (directed)	Use directed layout to show the orientation of the relationship between nodes. Communicate the strength of a relationship by the width and the direction of using arrow heads.

Questions:

- Who is closest to whom? Who is connected to whom?
- Who is the most popular? Who is the least?
- What communities exist and who are their members?
- What is the strength of the relationship between two entities?

Insight: see relationships, patterns, centrality, or interactions. This is shown by the width, color, or arrowheads on a line to communication relationships. The position of the nodes (that look like bubbles) show centrality in the network and distance from other nodes.

Data: edge lists or adjacency matrices show relationships between entities.

Chart options: undirected network diagram and directed network diagram.

Interview With a Practitioner

I interviewed Jack Hanlon from Jet.com who described how he uses data graphics in his practice.

 Kristen Sosulski (KS)   **Jack Hanlon (JH)**

KS:

Who are you and what do you do?

JH:

My name is Jack Hanlon. I started the Analytics & Insights (A&I) practice at Jet.com, where I serve on the management team. Our six teams in A&I are Customer Analytics, Marketing Analytics, Core Data Science, Research, Testing & Optimization, and Personalization. Our core belief is that if we can democratize access to insights, advance research and analysis techniques to all of Jet's employees, then Jet can create more amazing experiences for our customers and make stronger business decisions. That means our work involves everything from performing rigorous analysis, to doing in-person ethnographic studies every week, to teaching classes on things like Machine Learning, to creating large-scale user testing systems, to building pipes for data connections between systems. We want to be wherever information and automation create real impact.

KS:

How do you use data visualization in your practice?

JH:

Data visualization is critical for our practice to be successful, as it is one of the powerful mechanisms for storytelling. Most people's eyes glaze over if you discuss the different statistical methods in an analysis (even when this detail is critical), but if you create fantastic visuals with elite production value, you send a message about your credibility to support all the great work behind it. So, while we make sure our analytical methods are airtight, we also spend a great deal of time on data viz and other presentation skills because if you are a great storyteller, then you can make amazing things happen in an organization. In science, sometimes, we'd like to think that facts alone are sufficient, but time has shown how frequently that's not the case!

KS:

Can you share an example of how you have used data visualization in your practice? (show data graphic itself). What insight is evidenced by the graph provided? What did you do with that insight? (make a decision, inform policy, predict the future, etc.)

JH:

You can imagine how well the owner of a General Store knew their customers—getting to see each transaction and talk to every customer. One of the amazing things about eCom is the scale and access but it adds a few layers of abstraction between the consumer and the seller. As a result, we need to be able to understand what purchase patterns look like for certain customers to be able to make their lives easier wherever we can. In this case from 2015, right after the Jet launch, we wanted to see what categories of products were purchased together in the same cart, focused on consumable purchases (which are grocery-type items, e.g. items you would consume and have to replenish at some point like detergent or paper towels). Did they only buy other consumables? Did they also buy durables in that session (products that you don't need to replenish, like a bike or a shoe)?

The circles (nodes) represent item categories, and the colors represent whether the category contains consumables (in dark grey) or durables (in cyan). The categories purchased together are linked by lines (edges). The thickness of the lines indicates the frequency of the connections between the two categories, and the size of each circle represents its number of connections. Items that are frequently purchased together are attracted, while items that are infrequently purchased together are repelled.

In this image, we saw a number of categories that were categorized as durables based on our organizational structure but were purchased like consumables based on customer thinking. For example, light bulbs or printer ink/toner were both part of Electronics but are purchased like consumables. Similarly socks and underwear were part of Fashion, but their purchase pattern does not operate like blouses or shoes, and instead would be purchased with other consumables. This sounds obvious now, but like so many things—until it is illuminated in a digestible way—it can be easily missed. This insight enabled us to understand this concept of "shopping missions" that people are on when they come to us, which had tangible tactical implications including rethinking what products we should carry in certain warehouses (carrying these above products with consumables would allow them to ship together) and rethinking how we should think about merchandising on the site to make it easier to find the right products at the right time.

KS:

How did you create it? What was that data? What was the software? What would have been the alternative?

JH:

This is called a force-directed network diagram and it was created by Jamie Fitzgerald, a very talented data scientist in our group. She is a career scientist, so she spent a great deal of time working through understanding the data. She started simple with tables with number values indicating strength between categories, but due to the volume of data and the multiple connections for each item, it became clear that we needed a stronger relationship-focused and visual method to get the story across to the widest audience. From there it became clear that a graph-oriented method was the right approach. She explored a variety of graph-related options, both in terms of network diagram types, and of tools used to generate the graphs, and found that the easiest and most flexible option was Gephi, an open source software solution for visualizing and analyzing graphs and networks. When Jamie finished the first draft it was clear we were going to have something special here, and the larger version of this diagram that includes all categories and all colors is framed and hung outside of our central boardroom at the Jet. com HQ in Hoboken.

3.9 Chart Interface

Up until this point, we have assumed that we were creating static, motionless, unresponsive data graphics. Visualizations that serve as an interface to navigate or traverse data elements feature animated and interactive components.

3.9.1 ANIMATION

Animation charts show the movement of data encodings, such as bubbles, lines, points, lines, fills, nodes, or areas, in a sequence. There are three types of animations used in data visualizations: trend, transition and trace. These are used to show a succession of changes.

Trend Animation

A trend animation shows all trends simultaneously building up from beginning to end. For example, Table 3.10 shows a time series revealed gradually, point by point, using trend animation.

Table 3.10 A trend animation shown frame by frame

January	February	March

April	May	June

Transition Animation

A transition animation shows how a data point within an entire series changes. Usually, a point or series is highlighted throughout the animation to provide context for how the points around it change. Table 3.11 shows a transition animation of city budget by city and population and budget subcategory. The city in question is highlighted in gray. The position of the data point changes by movement along the x-axis.

Trace Animation

Trace animation uses fade-in and fade-out points or bubbles to show the direction of the flow of data points while keeping the historical data points present but faded. Too many data points can create a cluttered interface. Trace animation can be used to present variables related to geography over time. Table 3.12 shows a map of store openings over a six-year period. For each year, the store locations are represented in green; the points fade to a gray color as the animation moves to the next year in the sequence.

3.9.2 INTERACTION

Interactive data visualizations allow the audience to explore a data set through a visual interface. Users can manipulate and transform

Table 3.11 A transition animation shown frame by frame

Public Safety	Admin.	Community

Government	Public Works	Development

Table 3.12 A trace animation shown frame by frame

2013	2014	2015

2016	2017	2018

the output of the display through a variety of mouse actions. User actions include: select, explore, reconfigure, abstract/elaborate, filter, and connect (Ji Soo Yi, Youn ah Kang, Stasko, & Jacko, 2007). These actions differ from animation because: 1) the data is manipulated with the output being affected; or 2) the design of the visualization is transformed, which affects the presentation but not the data.

Select Interaction

The user marks one or more data points of interest (see Table 3.13). Click on a data point to mark or highlight it. This is used for tracking data points. For example, let's say we wanted to see the change in sales by store location over time. This can be illustrated in a bubble map (with bubbles sized by the sales). To see a particular store and sales, the data point is selected; through animation, the viewer sees how sales have changed for that store over time.

Explore Interaction

The user examines a subset of data through panning, zooming, or rotating the data graphic. Table 3.14 shows panning and zooming interactions on a point map of New York City.

Abstract and Elaborate Interaction

The user clicks on or hovers over a data point that reveals information. Table 3.15 presents a scatterplot with a point selected and a label with a description of the data point.

Reconfigure and Encode

The user can build interactive data graphics. For example, the user selects the variables to plot, determines the spatial arrangement of variables on the axes, and the visual appearance (size, shape, color, etc.). Figure 3.2 is a scatterplot with options to change the variables

Table 3.13 Marking a point of interest to highlight and observe

Click on data point	Data point changes color	Point size changes based on time or another attribute

Table 3.14 Exploring a point map using panning and zooming

Original view	Panning	Zooming	Selecting and zooming

Table 3.15 Clicking on or hovering over a data point reveals information

Original view	Hover or click
	Nuber of Rentals = 5,084 Humidity = .84

shown on the axes, the encoding type (circles, squares, or diamonds) and the color of the encoding (black, gray or blue).

Filter Interaction

The user changes the set of data items being presented based on some specific conditions. Filter types include a single value list, single value dropdown, single value slider, multiple values slider, multiple values list, multiple values dropdown, or search. See Table 3.16 for the common filter types.

Connect Interaction

Users interact with one data display to control the output of another data display. This is commonly used in dashboards. The connect action is used to highlight associations and relationships between data items that are already represented, and it shows hidden data items that are relevant to a specified item.

For example, Table 3.17 shows the original view and the data changes as the user clicks on the bubble.

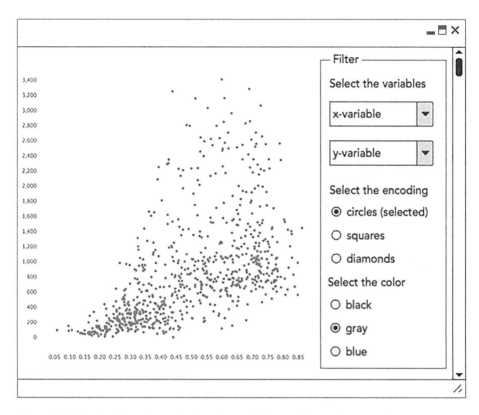

Figure 3.2 An interface for selecting the variables and encoding attributes

Table 3.16 Six types of filters

Single value list	Radio buttons	Drop down list
List item 1 List item 2 List item 3 List item 4 List item 5	○ option 1 ⦿ option 2 ○ option 3 ○ option 4	Select List item 1 List item 2 List item 3 List item 4
Checkbox	**Slider**	**Search**
☐ Checkbox 1 ☑ Checkbox 2 ☐ Checkbox 3 ☑ Checkbox 4 ☐ Checkbox 5		🔍 search

Table 3.17 An illustration of the connect interaction using one display (the bubbles) to control the output of the other displays (horizontal and vertical bar charts)

Original view

Hospital readmission and demographics

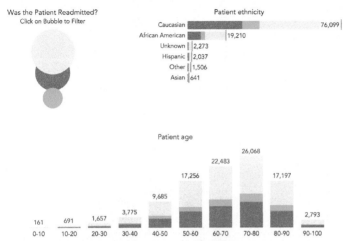

Source: UC Irvine Machine Learning Repository, _https://archive.ics.uci.edu/ml/datasets/Diabetes+130-US+hospitals+for+years+19.._

Dark gray bubble selected and series changes

Light gray bubble selected and series changes

Hospital readmission and demographics

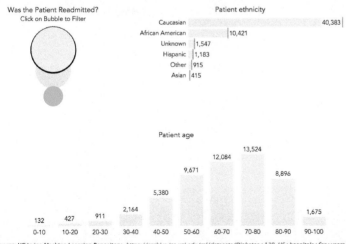

Source: UC Irvine Machine Learning Repository, _https://archive.ics.uci.edu/ml/datasets/Diabetes+130-US+hospitals+for+years+19.._

Green bubble selected and series changes

(Continued)

Table 3.17 (Continued)

Original view

Hospital readmission and demographics

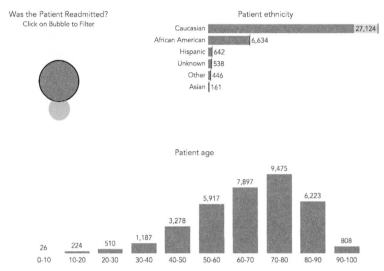

Was the Patient Readmitted?
Click on Bubble to Filter

Patient ethnicity

Patient age

Light gray bubble selected and series changes

Hospital readmission and demographics

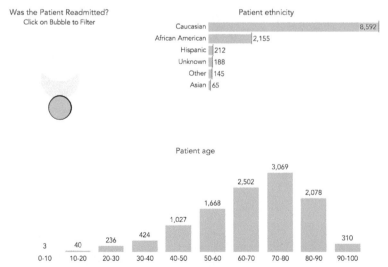

Was the Patient Readmitted?
Click on Bubble to Filter

Patient ethnicity

Patient age

Throughout this chapter, we looked at how the data type drives the types of visualizations available to reveal insights, including comparisons, distributions, compositions, relationships, locations, trends, connections, and sentiment.

Almost every chart can be transformed into one of three formats:

1. *Static*. Unanimated or non-interactive charts. The data may change or update with refreshed data, but the display does not change based on user actions.
2. *Animated*. Animated displays work well for projected displays or screen displays where a presenter is describing the insight shown on the screen. Use animation to guide the pathway through a chart. Animated displays can take several forms: transition animation, trend animation, or trace animation.
3. *Interactive*. Displays that are designed to allow users to explore a data set on their own—often providing details on a mouse over, giving different coordinated views, or panning and zooming.

3.10 Exercises

1. Download the data on motor vehicle accidents from New York Police Department from https://data.cityofnewyork.us/Public-Safety/NYPD-Motor-Vehicle-Collisions/h9gi-nx95. This data set contains geographic, categorical, and time series data.
   a. Create one display for each type of data to present an interesting insight.
   b. Create an animated time series display that shows the accidents in Manhattan over time.
   c. Create an interactive display that uses the borough as a filter for the location of accidents shown on the map.

Bibliography

The City of New York. (2014). Public recycling bins. Retrieved from https://data.cityofnewyork.us/Environment/Public-Recycling-Bins/sxx4-xhzg

Corum, J. (2011). The class of 2011. Retrieved from www.nytimes.com/interactive/2011/06/10/education/commencement-speeches-graphic.html

Ognyanova, K. (2016). Basic and advanced network visualization with R. Retrieved from www.kateto.net/wp-content/uploads/2016/04/Sunbelt%202016%20R%20Network%20Visualization%20Handout.pdf

Ribecca, S. (2013). The data visualisation catalogue. Retrieved from http://datavizcatalogue.com/index.html

Wong, D. M. (2010). *The Wall Street Journal guide to information graphics: The dos and don'ts of presenting data, facts, and figures.* New York, NY: W. W. Norton & Company.

Yi, J. S., Kang, Y., Stasko, J. T., & Jacko, J. A. (2007). Toward a deeper understanding of the role of interaction in information visualization. *IEEE Transactions on Visualization and Computer Graphics, 13*(6), 1224–1231. doi:10.1109/TVCG.2007.70515

IV

THE
DATA

How do you decode your data into information that
you can visually explore and analyze?

Consider your approach to the analysis of a new data set. At first, it can be a little intimidating to work with data you have never seen before.

When you begin any data project, there are some questions to keep in mind:

- What does your data represent in the real world? Where is it from? How was it collected?
- Who owns the data?
- How is this real-world phenomenon characterized by the data that you have? Specifically, what do the rows and columns mean?
- What time period is the data from?

Answering these questions will give you a working understanding of the data and how you can use it. Then, you can dig deeper and begin to format the data to facilitate the data exploration process. This involves preliminary data preparation, such as checking for missing values, renaming variables, and organizing the data in the correct form. Next, calculate descriptive statistics, such as the mean, median, maximum value, and minimum values. Data attributes can be visualized to show the shape of the data and highlight any anomalies. Now, you can move on to formulating questions that guide your data analysis and final visualizations.

Scenario

Imagine that your manager is thinking of sponsoring a bike-sharing program. She has given you a research task. You are charged with determining the preferences of people who rent bicycles through a popular bike-sharing program. Some questions that may drive your research include:

- What time of year is most popular for bike rentals?
- What's the most popular day of the week for bike rentals?
- What's the frequency of use for the average user?
- What are the most and least congested bike stations?

You have been asked by your manager to present your findings to the general staff in a simple presentation. You have never seen the data before. Where do you begin?

For any data project, following a few simple steps will enable you to transform your data into information (see Figure 4.1).

Figure 4.1 The process of decoding data into information

Let's go through the process of decoding the bike-sharing data into intelligible information.

4.1 UNDERSTAND YOUR DATA

First, you need to understand the data. The type of data you have will dictate the types of questions you ask to guide your analysis. To begin, look at your data. Data comes in file formats (see Table 4.1).

The most universal formats are comma-separated values (.csv), text (.txt), and Excel (.xlsx) files. These file types can be easily imported into most software used for data visualization such as Tableau, R, or Excel. See Chapter II–The Tools for data visualization software options.

In addition to these file formats, you may be working directly with data from a database (e.g., MySQL), a server, or from sophisticated software packages (e.g., SAS and SPSS), or other formats used for web-based data and meta data (e.g., HTML, JSON, and XML).

View the Data

Look at the data set presented in Table 4.2. This is a portion of the bike-sharing data from Capital Bikeshare[1] system in. csv format.

One of the first things you may notice is the number of rows and columns (the data dimensions). The data shown in Table 4.2 presents the first 10 rows of 731 and the first seven columns of 16. Rows are commonly referred to as "observations" or "records" and columns are described as "attributes" or "variables." For most visualization tasks, the data should be structured such that observations are stored in rows and variables are stored in columns. This is known as tidy data (Wickham, 2016).

The variable names listed in the first row of every column provide little information about the meaning of the values in each column. For example, look at the column named *season*. What is the meaning of season? What are the possible values for this variable? What type of variable is it?

You'll notice that in the *season* column the values are integers. The first 10 rows show a value of 1. However, the range in the full data set is between 1 and 4. What do the numbers represent? If we really think about it, it's unlikely that the numbers represent quantities. In fact, the

Table 4.1 Common data file formats and their attributes

File Format	Type of data	Structure	Application Support
.txt	Plain text	Lines of text	Notepad, TextEdit, Word, Excel
.csv	Plain text	Values separated by commas which form columns in a series of rows	Excel, Notepad, TextEdit
.xlsx	Formatted text, images, charts	Worksheets in Workbook	Excel

Bike sharing data

Table 4.2 A preview of the daily bike-sharing data from Capital Bikeshare

instant	dteday	season	yr	mnth	holiday	weekday
1	1/1/11	1	0	1	0	6
2	1/2/11	1	0	1	0	0
3	1/3/11	1	0	1	0	1
4	1/4/11	1	0	1	0	2
5	1/5/11	1	0	1	0	3
6	1/6/11	1	0	1	0	4
7	1/7/11		0	1	0	5
8	1/8/11	1	0	1	0	6
9	1/9/11	1	0	1	0	0
10	1/10/11	1	0		0	1

numbers represent the seasons of the year. The numbers (1 through 4) are probably a code for each of the four seasons of the year. Without additional information, such as a data dictionary or a README file, it would be impossible to know for certain that the values correspond to the seasons of the year. Furthermore, which seasons are coded as 1, 2, 3, or 4? This leads us to the next step, reviewing the data dictionary to better understand the meaning behind the values and the other variables.

Review the Data Dictionary

A data dictionary defines the characteristics of each variable. If your data comes from a reputable source (see Chapter V for a discussion on data integrity), odds are that it includes a data dictionary. The meaning of the variable *season* is defined in the data dictionary (Table 4.3).

Data Dictionary

Table 4.3 A snapshot of the data dictionary of the hourly bike sharing data from Capital Bikeshare

Field/Variable	Definition
instant	Record index
dteday	Date
season	Season (1: winter, 2: spring, 3: summer, 4: fall)
Yr	Year (0: 2011, 1: 2012)
Mnth	Month (1 to 12)
Hr	Hour (0 to 23)
holiday	Whether day is holiday or not (extracted from http://dchr.dc.gov/page/holiday-schedule)
weekday	Day of the week
workingday	1: If day is neither weekend nor holiday, 0: otherwise
weathersit	1: Clear, Few clouds, Partly cloudy; 2: Mist + Cloudy, Mist + Broken clouds, Mist + Few clouds, Mist; 3: Light snow, Light rain + Thunderstorm + Scattered clouds, Light Rain + Scattered clouds; 4: Heavy Rain + Ice Pellets + Thunderstorm + Mist, Snow + Fog
Temp	Normalized temperature in Fahrenheit
Atemp	Normalized feeling temperature in Fahrenheit
Hum	Normalized humidity. The values are divided to 100 (max)
windspeed	Normalized wind speed. The values are divided to 67 (max)
casual	Count of casual users
registered	Count of registered users
Cnt	Count of total rental bikes including both casual and registered

Season is a categorical variable defined by one of four values, each representing a season (1: winter, 2: spring, 3: summer, 4: fall). The variable *yr* is coded with the value of 0 for 2011 and 1 for 2012, rather than actual year value of 2011 or 2012. The variable *weathersit* is encoded with four possible values, 1 through 4. The values correspond to the daily weather situation as defined in Table 4.4.

In addition, the data dictionary shows the types of data such as date, categorical, and numeric data.

Date and Time

A date can take many formats including MM:DD:YYYY or MM/DD/YY. Some date formats include a time element such as hour (HH) or minute (MM). The field *dteday* is in MM/DD/YY format.

Table 4.4 The data dictionary for the variable *weathersit*

Value	Definition
1:	Clear, Few clouds, Partly cloudy
2:	Mist + Cloudy, Mist + Broken clouds, Mist + Few clouds, Mist
3:	Light snow, Light rain + Thunderstorm + Scattered clouds, Light Rain + Scattered clouds
4:	Heavy Rain + Ice Pellets + Thunderstorm + mist, Snow +Fog

Numeric Data

Numeric data can take the form of integers (positive or negative whole numbers) or floating-point decimals (positive or negative non-whole numbers). Integers are used for *cnt*, *registered*, and *casual* users per day. These obviously have to be whole numbers. Whereas decimals (also known as double or floating-point decimals) are used for the temperature variables: *temp*, *atemp*, and *hum*. Variables that are of type "numeric" enable mathematical manipulation.

Shouldn't all numbers be of type numeric?

The short answer is no. There are some numbers, such as product bar codes, years, dates, and identification numbers, that should be treated as characters or strings.

Categorical Data

Many of the variables in this data set are coded as categorical variables. This means that there is a non-numeric meaning to the numbers assigned to the variable. For example: *holiday*, *season*, and *weathersit*.

Other Data Types

There are other data types that are not included in the bike-sharing data dictionary. These include Boolean, geographical, and text data.

Boolean

Boolean data is a logical data type in which the values are either TRUE or FALSE. The variable holiday could easily be converted to a Boolean variable. Each 0 could be replaced with the value of FALSE and each 1 could be replaced with the value of TRUE.

Geographical

Geographical data includes zip codes, latitude, longitude, geocodes, states, countries, counties, airport codes, and U.S. census tracks.

Text

Variables with values that are text, such as *Country* in Table 4.6, are those types of data for which you cannot perform standard mathematical calculations (addition, multiplication, subtraction, etc.). These data are classified as text, strings, or characters.

Levels of Measurement

Each variable has a particular level of measurement related to the encoding of the data. Level of measurement "is a classification proposed in order to describe the nature of information contained within numbers assigned to objects or subjects, therefore within the variable" (Level of measurement, 2008, para 1). The well-known classification of measurement has four levels: nominal, ordinal, interval, and ratio (see Table 4.5). Nominal measurement uses categories such as 1, 2, 3, and 4 to refer to the season of the year. Ordinal measurement scales indicate a direction in addition to a category. The top-ranking MBA programs would be described by a number indicating its position within the total rankings as 1st, 2nd, 3rd, etc. Interval scales include data that are constructed with equal intervals, such as hour of the day or level of happiness, on an equal scale from 1 to 10. Ratio scales have an absolute zero point, such as age and salary. Data collected using a ratio scale allows for more complex quantitative analysis. The level of measurement for a variable limits the types of graphs, summary statistics, and analytic techniques that can be applied.

Analyzing and visualizing data without knowing the meaning of the variables makes data interpretation unreliable because you could only guess what the variables mean. By approaching a data visualization task informed about the data and its attributes, you can better formulate questions for visual exploration. The next step is to prepare the data for analytical and visualization tasks.

4.2 PREPARING YOUR DATA

Preparing your data for analysis involves appropriately structuring it for easy processing, renaming the column names for readability and usability, and checking the integrity of the data.

Levels of Measurement

Table 4.5 Levels of measurement

Nominal	Nominal measurement is like using categorical levels of variables that refer to classifications rather than quantities.
Meal Preference	Breakfast, Lunch, Dinner
Religious Affiliation	1=Buddhist, 2=Muslim, 3=Christian, 4=Jewish, 5=Other
Political Orientation	Republican, Democratic, Libertarian, Green
Ordinal	An ordinal scale indicates direction, in addition to providing nominal information.
Rank	1st place, 2nd place, . . . last place
Level of agreement	Strongly disagree, disagree, somewhat disagree. . .
Interval	Scales constructed with equal intervals.
Time of day	On a 12-hour clock, 1:00pm, 2:00pm, 3:00pm
Level of happiness	Rated from 1 to 10, with 1 being the lowest.
Ratio	A ratio scale has an absolute zero point. Using a ratio scale permits comparisons, such as being twice as high, or one-half as much.
Years of work experience	1,2,3
Income	$150,000. . .
Number of children	1,2,3
GPA: grade point average	3.0, 3.1

Structure the Data

The rows should correspond to observations and the columns should correspond to the observed variables. This makes it easier to map the data to visual properties such as position, color, size, or shape.

Look at Table 4.6. Are the variables in columns and observations in rows?

In this case, the observations are in columns, one value for each year. Years are coded as variables. This wide-data format makes visualizing this time series difficult. Why? What if you wanted to show the change

World Internet Usage per 100 People

Table 4.6 World Internet Usage per 100 People

Country	2000	2001	2002	2003	2004
China	1.78	2.64	4.60	6.20	7.30
Mexico	5.08	7.04	11.9	12.90	14.10
Panama	6.55	7.27	8.52	9.99	11.14
Senegal	0.40	0.98	1.01	2.10	4.39
Singapore	36.00	41.67	47.00	53.84	62.00
United Arab Emirates	23.63	26.27	28.32	29.48	30.13
United States	43.08	49.08	58.79	61.7	64.76

Source: World Bank, 2013

over time for all seven countries? Which variables would you map to the x-axis and y-axis?

Create a time series chart using the World Internet Usage data in wide format available at: http://becomingvisual.com/portfolio/wideandlongformats. Note the challenges associated with this data format for graphing.

If you tried graphing the data as a time series, you might have produced something similar to the chart in Figure 4.2. This produces an odd-looking chart that maps each country as a line, including the column name *Country*, encoded years on the x-axis using the numbers 1 through 13 instead of 2000 through 2013. Notice that the y-axis's scale has a large range because the years 2000 through 2013 are plotted as values, making the *Country* line appear well above the lines for China, Mexico, etc.

When data is transformed into a long format, as in Table 4.7, it is possible to graph a time series chart (see Figure 4.3). The variable *year* is plotted on the x-axis, *usage* is on the y-axis for every country and every year. Each *country* is encoded as a separate line.

If you return to the bike-sharing data, you can easily see that the data is formatted correctly; observations are in rows and variables in columns.

For example, to visualize the temperature by day, plot the *dteday* variable on the x-axis and the *temp* on the y-axis (see Figure 4.4). Time-series charts allow us to quickly spot patterns in the data. In the example, temperature has a seasonal behavior.

World Internet Usage per 100 People

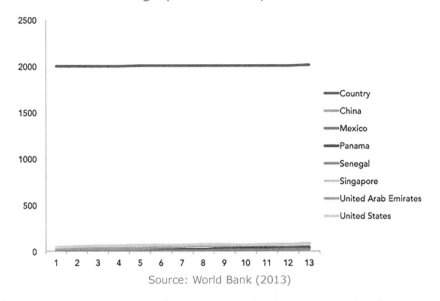

Source: World Bank (2013)

Figure 4.2 An attempt to graph a time series data set in a wide-data format using Microsoft Excel

Table 4.7 Data in long format

country	year	usage
China	2000	1.78
Mexico	2000	5.08
Panama	2000	6.55
Senegal	2000	0.40
Singapore	2000	36.0
United Arab Emirates	2000	23.63
United States	2000	43.08
China	2001	2.64
Mexico	2001	7.04
Panama	2001	7.27
Senegal	2001	0.98
Singapore	2001	41.67
United Arab Emirates	2001	26.27
United States	2001	49.08
China	2002	4.60

Since 2011, the UAE has surpassed Singapore and the United States in the number of people with Internet per 100 people.

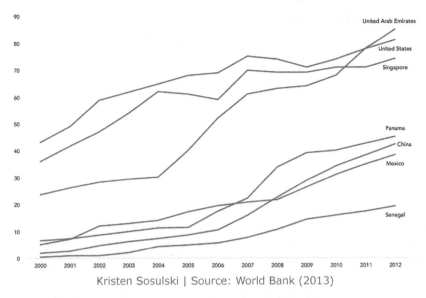

Kristen Sosulski | Source: World Bank (2013)

Figure 4.3 Graph of a time series data set in a long format

Temperature by day (in degrees Fahrenheit)

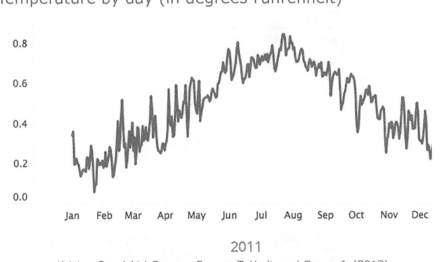

2011

Kristen Sosulski | Source: Fanaee-T, Hadi, and Gama, J. (2013)

Figure 4.4 A time series of day and temperature

Survey Data

Data collected from surveys or opinion polls tend to require additional processing and formatting to allow for easy analysis. Table 4.8 shows responses from a survey. The questions are formatted as columns and the responses are formatted as rows. This wide format makes it difficult to create charts that group the scales—very good, good, average, poor, very poor, and no knowledge—for each question.

Most visualization software will have difficulty visualizing much of this data unless it is transformed into a different structure. Even sophisticated packages, such as Tableau, will limit the visualizations to a single question in order to produce a chart similar to Figure 4.5.

With this type of survey data, we want to show an aggregate of the responses to each question, not how an individual responded. We want to answer questions such as what percentage of students rated their competence in Tableau as *very good?* We want to produce with ease a chart, such as Figure 4.5, organized by *question* and *response percentage*.

How many variables are required to plot the percentage of responses by response category per question? There are 10 questions and six possible responses per question. We will need to create a table that looks like Table 4.9. For details on how to transform the data in Table 4.8 to Table 4.9, go to http://becomingvisual.com/portfolio/summarytable

Table 4.8 Survey data

Respondent	Question 1: Excel	Question 2: Tableau	Question 3: Photoshop	Question 4: PowerPoint	Question 5: Google Charts
1	Good	Very Good	No knowledge	Good	No knowledge
2	Good	Good	Good	Very Good	No knowledge
3	Very Good	Average	No knowledge	Very Good	No knowledge
4	Very Good	Very Good	Poor	Very Good	Good
5	Average	Poor	No knowledge	Average	Average
6	Very Good	Poor	No knowledge	Very Good	No knowledge
7	Good	Poor	No knowledge	Very Good	No knowledge
8	Good	Poor	Poor	Very Good	Poor
9	Good	Poor	Poor	Good	No knowledge

How do you rate your skills in R programming?

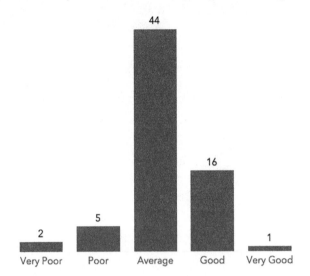

Figure 4.5 Graphing a single question from the survey data with responses on the x-axis and count of response by question on the y-axis

Table 4.9 A summary table

Question	Very Good	Good	Average	Poor	Very Poor	No Knowledge
Excel	42.65%	44.12%	11.76%	1.47%	0	0
Tableau	7.35%	20.59%	41.18%	25.00%	5.88%	0
Photoshop	2.94%	5.88%	16.18%	29.41%	4.41%	41.18%
PowerPoint	48.53%	36.76%	14.71%	0	0	0
Google Charts	0	13.24%	27.94%	7.35%	2.94%	48.53%
JavaScript	0	2.94%	11.76%	16.18%	11.76%	57.35%
HTML	1.47%	5.88%	20.59%	14.71%	14.71%	42.65%
CSS	0	5.88%	11.76%	19.12%	7.35%	55.88%
R	1.47%	23.53%	64.71%	7.35%	2.94%	0
Python	1.47%	8.82%	27.94%	38.24%	23.53%	0

Table 4.9 provides you with summary data you need to create most data graphics, including bar, radar, and pie charts. For example, the data from this table was grouped into four basic technology skills category types to plot the radar chart in Figure 4.6.

Students know basic data tools best. However, they are less skilled in advanced data tools and least skilled in web design.

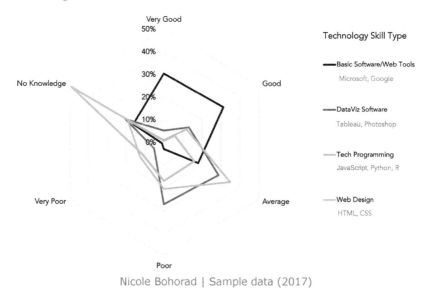

Nicole Bohorad | Sample data (2017)

Figure 4.6 Radar chart that shows the technical skills of the survey respondents

Try using the data in Table 4.9 to create a radar chart, bar chart and pie chart. Download the data at: http://becomingvisual.com/portfolio/summarytable

RENAME THE VARIABLES

Now that you are familiar with the data and the meaning of the variables, rename them to make the data more usable for data analysis and presentation. For example, the variable named *mnth* can be easily renamed *month* to make it more readable. Renaming variables is usually a manual process that requires you to change each column name. It is best practice to use lower case lettering and avoid spaces and hyphenation. See Table 4.10 for the renamed columns for the bike-sharing data set.

IDENTIFY MISSING VALUES

If your data contains missing values, you have to decide to either 1) leave out the select observations from your analysis, or 2) replace the missing data through data imputation.

Table 4.10 Bike-sharing data with the variables renamed

Old column names						
instant	dteday	season	yr	mnth	holiday	weekday
New column names						
instance	date	season	year	month	holiday	weekday
1	1/1/11	1	0	1	0	6
2	1/2/11	1	0	1	0	0
3	1/3/11	1	0	1	0	1
4	1/4/11	1	0	1	0	2
5	1/5/11	1	0	1	0	3
6	1/6/11	1	0	1	0	4
7	1/7/11		0	1	0	5
8	1/8/11	1	0	1	0	6
9	1/9/11	1	0	1	0	0
10	1/10/11	1	0		0	1

For example, in Table 4.11, there are two missing values for two observations.

1. Ignore any record with missing values.

   One strategy is to ignore the record with missing values and omit it from the data set.
   Pros: simple in implementation.
   Cons: if the majority of the data set contains missing values, this approach could lead to drastic reduction in the observations available for analysis in the data set.

2. Replace empty fields with a pre-defined value.

A second strategy is to define a value for every attribute that is missing a value. For each missing value, the pre-defined value will be substituted for it. A data analyst can draw assumptions from the data set to make an appropriate guess, or can substitute "NA" to signify a missing value in the data set. For example, in Table 4.11, the missing values are highlighted for row 7, column 3, and row 10, column 5 for the variables *season* and *month*, respectively. In these two cases, it is easy to replace the value with a pre-defined value. In row 7, we see that the season is winter based on the date field. Furthermore, in row 10, the month can be determined based on the date field as well. We would not want to ignore

There are many options for replacing missing values. These include 1) replacing empty fields with the values that appear most frequently, 2) using the mean value, or 3) developing a predictive model to determine with a degree of confidence and accuracy the best approximate value for the missing one.
Learn more at: http://becomingvisual.com/portfolio/missingfields

these records because the values can be easily determined. The missing values are replaced with pre-defined values as shown in Table 4.12.

Pros: observations are not omitted, and the full data set can be used.
Cons: if the data set has many missing values, it may be difficult to determine all the missing data values.

Table 4.11 Observing missing values in the data set

instance	date	season	year	month	holiday	weekday
1	1/1/11	1	0	1	0	6
2	1/2/11	1	0	1	0	0
3	1/3/11	1	0	1	0	1
4	1/4/11	1	0	1	0	2
5	1/5/11	1	0	1	0	3
6	1/6/11	1	0	1	0	4
7	1/7/11		0	1	0	5
8	1/8/11	1	0	1	0	6
9	1/9/11	1	0	1	0	0
10	1/10/11	1	0		0	1

Table 4.12 The empty fields replaced with values

Instance	date	season	year	month	holiday	weekday
1	1/1/11	1	0	1	0	6
2	1/2/11	1	0	1	0	0
3	1/3/11	1	0	1	0	1
4	1/4/11	1	0	1	0	2
5	1/5/11	1	0	1	0	3
6	1/6/11	1	0	1	0	4
7	1/7/11	1	0	1	0	5
8	1/8/11	1	0	1	0	6
9	1/9/11	1	0	1	0	0
10	1/10/11	1	0	1	0	1

Generally, if the number of cases of missing values is extremely small, then omitting the values from the analysis may be appropriate. A general rule is if the number of cases with missing values is 5% or less, then omitting them from the analysis may not drastically affect the results. It may be possible to use inference or a predictive model to estimate the values.

4.3 Compute Descriptive Statistics

Descriptive statistics are the numbers and calculations used to help summarize raw data (Wheelan, 2013). They provide information about the distribution, the median, minimum, maximum values, variance, and standard deviation. Descriptive statistics can also help frame a problem. They give the context of the selected values to the entire data set. For instance, they may help to identify outliers and correlations between variables.

Table 4.13 shows the mean, median, minimum, and maximum values for each variable in the bike-sharing data set. This is particularly useful for continuous variables such as *temp*, *cnt*, *casual*, and *registered*. For example, you can easily see the average number of customers (casual and registered) per day. The minimum and maximum values are useful for understanding the range for the high and low temperatures.

Descriptive statistics for bike-sharing data set:

Table 4.13 Basic descriptive statistics calculated for the bike sharing data set

	vars	n	mean	standard deviation	median	min	max	range
instant	1	731	366.00	211.17	366.00	1.00	731.00	730.00
dteday	2	731	NaN	NA	NA	Inf	−Inf	−Inf
season	3	731	2.50	1.11	3.00	1.00	4.00	3.00
year	4	731	0.50	0.50	1.00	0.00	1.00	1.00
mnth	5	731	6.52	3.45	7.00	1.00	12.00	11.00
holiday	6	731	0.03	0.17	0.00	0.00	1.00	1.00
weekday	7	731	3.00	2.00	3.00	0.00	6.00	6.00
workingday	8	731	0.68	0.47	1.00	0.00	1.00	1.00
weathersit	9	731	1.40	0.54	1.00	1.00	3.00	2.00
temp	10	731	0.50	0.18	0.50	0.06	0.86	0.80
atemp	11	731	0.47	0.16	0.49	0.08	0.84	0.76
hum	12	731	0.63	0.14	0.63	0.00	0.97	0.97
windspeed	13	731	0.19	0.08	0.18	0.02	0.51	0.49
casual	14	731	848.18	686.62	713.00	2.00	3410.00	3408.00
registered	15	731	3656.17	1560.26	3662.00	20.00	6946.00	6926.00
Cnt	16	731	4504.35	1937.21	4548.00	22.00	8714.00	8692.00

Calculate descriptive statistics in a snap.
Use R's summary function. Or, Excel users can go to data > data analysis. Mac users may have a little more difficulty unless they download the Stat-Plus add-on for Excel. Learn more at: http://becomingvisual.com/portfolio/summarystatistics

Table 4.14 Some methods of exploration through visualization

Metric	Purpose	How to
Summary Statistics Mean, max, min,	To show the average, largest, smallest values, shape of the data	Density plot, histogram, boxplots
Correlation	To show the degree to which a change in x impacts y	Scatterplot or scatterplot matrix with trend line
Year over year	To show percentage change difference from one year to the next	Bar chart, line chart (and tool tip)
Moving average	Trend or lagging indicator to smooth out the noise/fluctuations over a distinct time period	Use dual axis chart for moving average series
Cluster	In an unsupervised way, to identify the similar members and group them accordingly	Use a scatterplot and scatter plot matrix + cluster, use a map + cluster for geospatial data

4.4. Explore the Data Visually

There are several ways you can visually explore data. The method of exploration is determined by the metric used, such as the mean or moving average. See Table 4.14.

There are a few simple statistical visualizations that are useful for data exploration and understanding. These include the histogram, boxplot, and scatterplot.

1. Histograms

Histograms are simply graphical frequency distribution tables. A histogram looks like a bar chart, but values are grouped into bins. To build a histogram, a single variable goes on the x-axis. Each bar represents a bin. The bins' sizes are determined by the visualization software automatically, but they can also be set manually.

As a first step, you could graph a histogram to display the shape of a distribution of a single variable, such as number of rentals. The histogram in Figure 4.7 shows the shape of the data for the number of rentals per day in 2012. Each bar represents the number of days by the sum of rentals per day for the given bin or range. To capture the viewer's attention, a different color in the histogram is used to highlight a relevant bin. For example, the green bar shows that there were 37 days where rentals were between 7,275 and 7,555.

2. Boxplots

A boxplot displays the distribution of values of a single variable along an axis. It shows the range of values. The two rectangles demarcate the middle 50% of the data, known as the interquartile range (IQR). The median or middle value is shown between the two boxes. The dots represent each data point. See Figure 4.8 for an example of 12 boxplots, one for each month of the year.

3. Scatterplots

To see relationships, scatterplots are useful. We look for positive or negative correlations to aid in decision making. For example, can you predict y from x or the number of rentals on a particular day when the temperature is 45 degrees?

Frequency of bicycle rentals in 2012

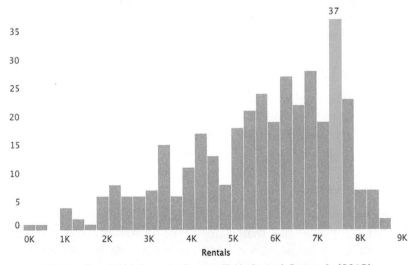

Kristen Sosulski | Source: Fanaee-T, Hadi, and Gama, J. (2013)

Figure 4.7 A histogram of the total daily rentals in 2012

Boxplot of bicycle rentals by month in 2012

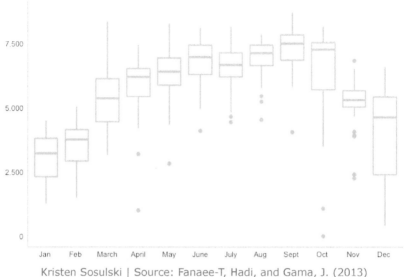

Kristen Sosulski | Source: Fanaee-T, Hadi, and Gama, J. (2013)

Figure 4.8 A boxplot of the total number of rentals in 2012

In Figure 4.9, the chart shows that there is a positive correlation between temperature and the total number of bike rides. However, when temperatures peak above 80 degrees, we see a decrease.

To see the relationships between every combination of two variables within a data set, use a scatterplot matrix (see Figure 4.10).

4. Year Over Year

The year over year metric is useful for showing the percentage change from one year to the next. In Figure 4.11, the percentage change from one year to the next is shown by month. For example, the change in bike rentals from January 2011 to January 2012 was 153.3%.

5. Moving Average

Moving average analysis is used to smooth out fluctuations or noise in the price, for example, over a period of time. A moving average is a lagging indicator because it is based on past data. It is a metric that is not relevant to the bike-sharing data, but very relevant to stock prices.

Relationship between temperature and bicycle rentals

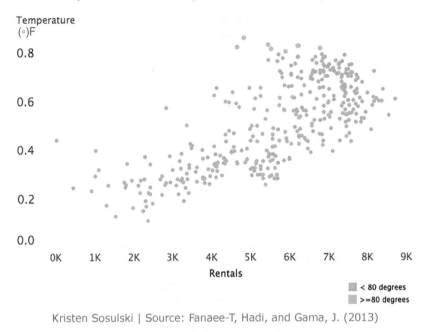

Kristen Sosulski | Source: Fanaee-T, Hadi, and Gama, J. (2013)

Figure 4.9 A scatterplot that shows the relationship between the rentals and temperature in 2012

For example, Figure 4.12 shows the close price of Apple Inc., denoted by the gray line. The five-day moving average is shown with the green line. In this example, a declining moving average indicates that it is in a downtrend in the stock price. A rising moving average indicates an uptrend.

6. Clusters

Clustering is a data-mining approach used to identify undefined groupings in a data set and group them accordingly. Let's assume the groupings are determined by those observations with similar means. Then, the groups or clusters can be visualized and analyzed. For example, in Figure 4.13, each cluster of observations can be distinguished by a different color. This is approach is used to see if there are groupings within the data. The similar items are shown as being closer together and those that are dissimilar are shown as farther apart. Cluster analysis is a simple function built into many business intelligence tools; however, the underlying algorithm is quite complex.

What affects bicycle rentals?

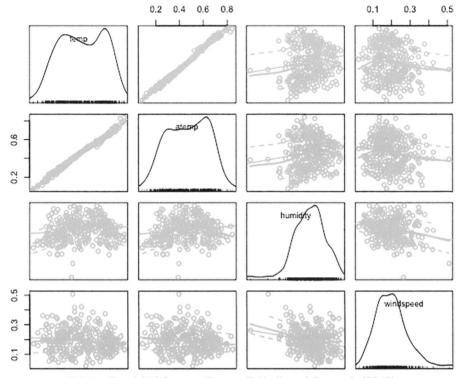

Kristen Sosulski | Source: Fanaee-T, Hadi, and Gama, J. (2013)

Figure 4.10 A scatterplot matrix that shows the relationship between each variable shown

You can save time by creating a scatterplot matrix that shows the relationships between many variables in a single data set as shown in Figure 4.10. Learn more at: http://becomingvisual.com/portfolio/scatterplotmatrix

4.5 Devise the Problem, Challenge, and/or Questions

At this point in the process, you should have gained enough insight to frame a question that guides the rest of your analysis. Sometimes, you don't know what to ask of your data, and other times, your questions cannot be answered by the data you have. In most visual analytical explorations, there will be a back and forth between defining the questions and identifying the data sources that contain the information you need.

A breakdown of bicycle rental growth from 2011 to 2012 by month

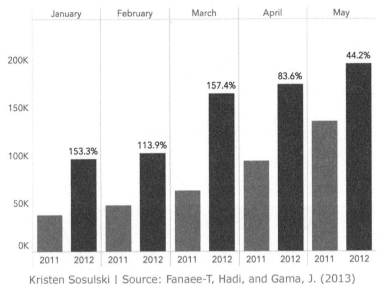

Kristen Sosulski | Source: Fanaee-T, Hadi, and Gama, J. (2013)

Figure 4.11 Year over year percentage change in bicycle rentals categorized by month

Often, your question will fall into one of three categories: Past, present, or future.

Some questions that can guide a historical analysis of past events are:

- Do weather conditions affect rental behaviors?
- Does the precipitation, day of week, season, hour of the day, etc. affect rental behavior?
- Which weather conditions affect behavior the most? Do they differ by season?

These questions generally serve to guide reports when the analyst is reporting on past events.

A question based on the present is:

How many bikes were rented in the past hour or today?

This type of question is reserved for producing a chart of a current state of an event. The data we are using cannot answer this question because it is historical data from 2011 and 2012.

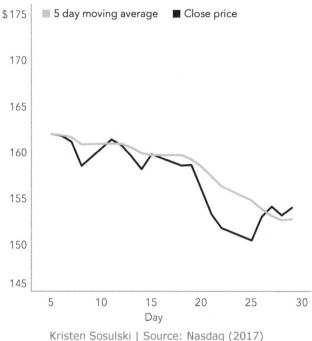

Apple's close price and five-day moving average

Kristen Sosulski | Source: Nasdaq (2017)

Figure 4.12 Illustration of Apple Inc.'s five-day moving average and closing stock price

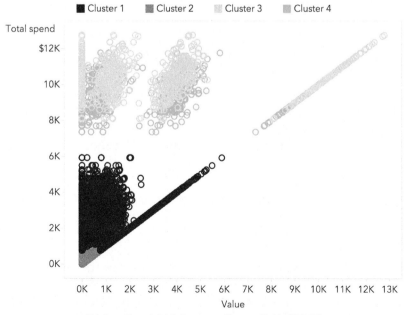

Kristen Sosulski | Source: Chernoff, H. (2017)

Figure 4.13 A data graphic of a cluster analysis

A question about the future could be framed as:

Will bike rentals be higher in the summer than in the winter due to weather?

Questions about the future involve analysis that requires prediction or forecasting methods. The analyst in this case is trying to predict the future from past data. This may involve the use of data-mining models, statistics models such as logistic regression (for discrete outcomes that are dichotomous (0, 1–absent or present)).

4.6 Exercises

1. As a next step, try to create visualizations that answer the following questions:
    -   What are the rentals by year and customer type?
    -   What is the most popular day for bike rentals? Does it differ by season, year, or by customer type?
    -   How does the weather affect rentals?
2. Select a data set from one of the resources provided at: http://becomingvisual.com/portfolio/findingdata. Go through the process of 1) understanding your data; 2) preparing the data for analysis and visualization; 3) computing descriptive statistics; 4) exploring the data visually and devising the problem challenge; and 5) questions to guide your data analysis.

Note

1   Fanaee-T, Hadi, and Gama, Joao. (2013). 'Event Labeling Combining Ensemble Detectors and Background Knowledge'. *Progress in Artificial Intelligence*. Pages. 1–15. Berlin Heidelberg: Springer.

Bibliography

Bernard, M., Lida, B., Riley, S., Hackler, T., & Janzen, K. (2002). A comparison of popular online fonts: Which size and type is best? Retrieved from http://usabilitynews.org/a-comparison-of-popular-online-fonts-which-size-and-type-is-best/

Calkins, K. G. (2005). Definitions, uses, data types, and levels of measurement. Retrieved from www.andrews.edu/~calkins/math/edrm611/edrm01.htm#DATA_TYPE

Chernoff, H. (2017). Casino player dataset.

Fanaee-T, H., & Game, J. (2013). Event labeling combining ensemble detectors and background knowledge. *Progress in Artificial Intelligence*, 1–15. Retrieved from http://dx.doi.org/10.1007/s13748-013-0040-3

Level of measurement. (2008). In W. Kirch (Ed.), *Encyclopedia of public health* (pp. 851–852). Dordrecht, The Netherlands: Springer. Retrieved from https://link.springer.com/referenceworkentry/10.1007%2F978-1-4020-5614-7_1971 on April 1, 2018

Nasdaq. Apple Inc. common stock quote and summary data. Retrieved from www.nasdaq.com/symbol/aapl on June 1, 2017

Paradi, D. (2017). Using graphs and tables on presentation slides. Retrieved from www.thinkoutsidetheslide.com/using-graphs-and-tables-on-presentation-slides/

Publication manual of the American Psychological Association. (2010). (6th ed., repr. ed.). Washington, DC: American Psychological Association.

Wheelan, C. J. (2013). *Naked statistics* (1st ed.). New York, NY: W. W. Norton & Company.

Wickham, H., & Grolemund, G. (2016). *R for data science* (1st ed.). O'Reilly Media. Retrieved from http://proquestcombo.safaribooksonline.com/9781491910382

Zimmer, J. (2010). PowerPoint math: The 1-6-6 rule. Retrieved from https://mannerofspeaking.org/2010/03/04/powerpoint-math-the-1-6-6-rule/

V

THE
DESIGN

How do you design readable and clear data graphics?

Look at Figure 5.1 Is the following statement true or false?

From 2012 to 2016, Jamaica's rural population did not grow.

The answer is true. The rural population did not grow. In fact, the rural population has steadily declined since 2002. If you answered FALSE, you are not alone. I ran a simple experiment with Amazon's Mechanical Turk Workers.[1] They were shown the same chart and only 64% answered the question correctly. Approximately one-third of the audience interpreted the data insight incorrectly.

What makes this chart difficult to read?

The data was encoded into bars above the baseline. This makes it harder to see the decrease in population from 2012 through 2016.

Jamaica's rural population growth (percentage) from 2000 to 2016

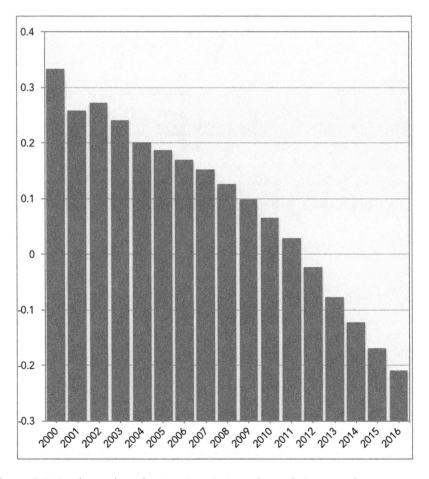

Figure 5.1 A column chart showing Jamaica's rural population growth

Table 5.1 clearly shows the decrease with negative values. Showing the bars above the baseline created an illusion that the population was growing. When the chart was modified to plot the negative values below the baseline, the decline is easier to spot (see Figure 5.2).

This example illustrates that a simple design decision (keeping the bars above the baseline) can affect chart readability and reader comprehension. There are several other differences between the design aesthetics in Figure 5.1 and Figure 5.2. Specifically, in Figure 5.1, note the non-data elements of the chart:

- bolded and italicized lettering for the chart title;
- a gray frame border around the area;
- a gray rectangular border around the chart;
- horizontal gridlines;
- a light gray filled chart background;
- a shadow behind the vertical bars;
- tick marks on the x-axis and y-axis;
- angled text label on x-axis; and
- absence of reference to the data source, year, and chart author.

Each of these design choices can affect the chart's message.

Do you think Figure 5.4 shows the decline in population more clearly? Given that showing the decline is the objective, the line chart is a better choice.

Table 5.1 A table showing the percentage growth of Jamaica's rural population from 2006 through 2016.

Year	Annual growth
. . .	. . .
2006	0.169870093
2007	0.152267345
2008	0.126366698
2009	0.099412063
2010	0.065785007
2011	0.029922845
2012	−0.022940047
2013	−0.07668403
2014	−0.123093677
2015	−0.168365624
2016	−0.209235742

Source: World Bank (2016)

Jamaica's rural population growth (percentage) from
2000 through 2016

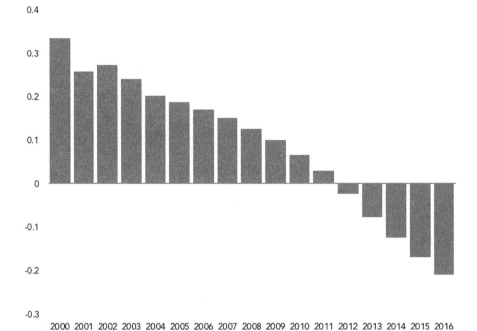

Kristen Sosulski | Source: World Bank (2017)

Figure 5.2 A column chart showing Jamaica's rural population growth with the negative values below the baseline

The available data dictates the chart type that best presents the data visually. For example, to show Jamaica's declining rural population on a map, specific geospatial data (latitude and longitude) are required. However, the World Bank (2017) only provides the percentage of growth defined as the *difference between the total population and the urban population*.

How would you present Jamaica's changing rural population? Download the data from http://becomingvisual.com/portfolio/jamaica and create your own data graphic.

In addition, the medium (website, paper, projector, laptop, mobile devices, television, etc.) limits the options for interaction, animation, narration, and space to present the visualization. For example,

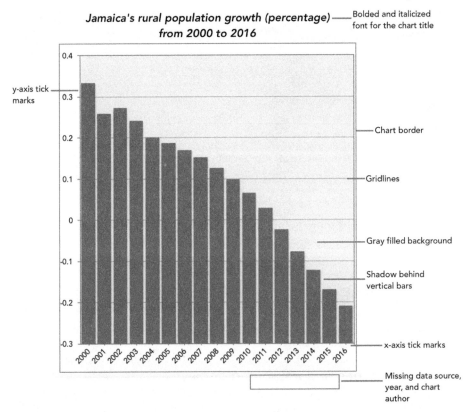

Figure 5.3 A chart that highlights some of the design decisions regarding the non-data elements in a chart

animated displays are impossible for printed charts, and interactive visualizations are only possible with computer-based charts. Your design decisions affect final output and your audience's perception of your insight.

This chapter focuses on design decisions that can affect the efficacy of data visualizations. There are some simple, core design standards applicable to every chart.

5.1 Design Standards

There are 10 key design standards. They enable creation of readable and interpretable data graphics. Many of the standards are based on the work of leaders in the field of information visualization, including Edward Tufte (1990, 1997, 2001), Dona Wong (2010), and Stephen Few (2012).

Since 2012, Jamaica's rural population has been on a steady decline.

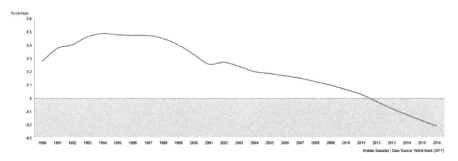

Figure 5.4 A line chart showing the decline in Jamaica's rural population

#1 CHART FORMAT

Optimize the Data Graphic Quality for the Right Platform

The resolution and file types differ for printed publications, projected slide presentations, and web-based displays.

Paper publications: for printed charts, determine how the chart will look in grayscale and in color. It should be readable in both. Consider the paper grade and finish. Save charts using high resolution for best printing quality. The ideal resolution is 300 dots per inch (dpi). The file type should be TIFF, EPS, PSD, or PDF. Position the chart within the margins of the page. Always include a caption and a reference to the data source.

Web-based displays: for static data graphics presented on a web page, use a minimum resolution of 150 ppi (pixels per inch). The SVG (vector graphics) file type allows you to view an image on multiple devices and platforms with different screen resolutions. For interactive data graphics, format the text and numbers for tool tips and data points that reveal information upon mouse over.

Projected slide presentations: for projected displays, determine how the chart will look on a large screen. The minimum resolution is 150 ppi. Use PNG-24 for the highest image quality. If the data graphic is interactive or animated, it may need modifications to support readability on a larger screen. Consider taking a screen recording of the animation or interactive data graphic and embedding it in PowerPoint. Set the screen dimensions to 2280 x 1800. Save the recording as an mp4 file. An alternative is to create several static images on separate slides in PowerPoint to simulate the animation, frame by frame.

Refer to Chapter VII–THE PRESENTATION for further guidance on using data graphics in presentations.

#2 COLOR

Use color only when it corresponds to differences in the data. Reserve color for highlighting a single data point or for differentiating a data series. Avoid thematic or decorative presentations. For example, avoid using red and green together. Be cognizant of the cultural meanings of the colors you select and the impact they may have on your audience.

Ensure high contrast values for colors. Allow even those with a color vision deficiency or color blindness to distinguish the different shades by using contrasting colors. Convert graphs to grayscale or print them out in black and white to test contrast.

Chart A in Figure 5.5 shows green and gray-stacked bars. These are converted to grayscale in Chart B. Note the lack of contrast between the green and gray values. When converted to grayscale, the differences between Region 1 and Region 2 are obscured. Chart C (see Figure 5.7) uses a deeper color gray for Region 1. This adds contrast when compared to Region 1.

#3 TEXT AND LABELS

Add a description that guides readers in interpreting your visualization. For example, see Figure 5.6. If you present a chart, include the description in the title or in your notes. This will ensure you communicate the key insight to the audience. Refer to Chapter VIII for more details on presentations with charts.

Explain your encodings. Specifically, what do the lines, points, bubbles, or bars mean?

There are multiple positive and negative cultural meanings for the color red. Learn more at: http://becomingvisual.com/portfolio/colormeaning

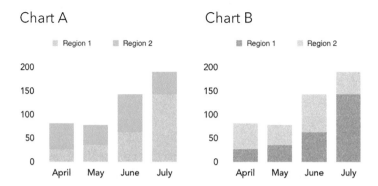

Figure 5.5 Chart A shows a low contrast stacked bar chart, and Chart B shows A's grayscale conversion.

Since 2012, Jamaica's rural population has been on a steady decline, which may signal a move to urban centers for better access to resources.

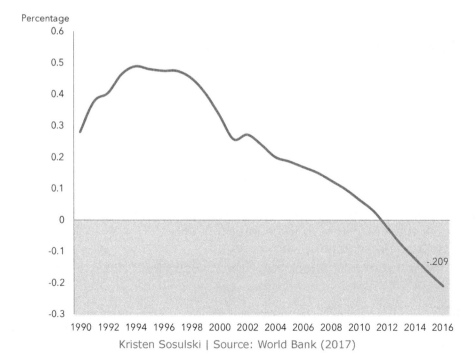

Kristen Sosulski | Source: World Bank (2017)

Figure 5.6 A chart with the data insight shown visually and communicated in text

When there are few data points, place the data labels directly on the data. Use a legend or an axis label when the chart encodings are too small to label (e.g., small points on a scatterplot). Don't label data points if readability is impeded as a result (see Figure 5.7, Chart A). Chart B labels select data points. Label data points you want your audience to identify. In Chart C, the axis is needed to identify the value of

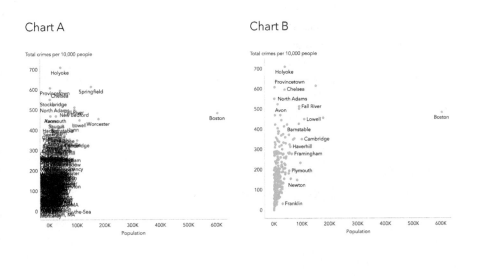

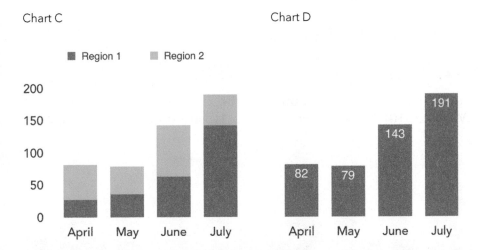

Figure 5.7 Chart A shows a scatterplot with every point labeled with text. Chart B shows the labeling of select data points. Chart C is a stacked bar chart using the y-axis to show the values for each bar, while values are labeled directly in Chart D

each bar. In Chart D, the data values for each bar segment are labeled directly on the bars.

#4 READABILITY

The font face, size, direction, and color affect the legibility. Which x-axis is easier to read in Figure 5.8? Chart C shows text presented as you would expect it—horizontally. Avoid setting text vertically or at an angle. Also, limit the use of italicized and bold-faced font. This inhibits readability when used in abundance.

Ensure everything on your chart is readable. Reminder: If you are using a chart in a PowerPoint presentation, use a larger font size for axis labels, scales, data labels, and the chart title. Refer to Chapter VII—THE PRESENTATION for further guidance.

#5 SCALES

Use natural increments for x-axis and y-axis scales such as:

0, 1, 2, 3, 4, 5
0, 2, 4, 6, 8, 10
0, 10, 20, 30, 40
0, 25, 50, 75, 100
0, 100, 200, 300, 400
0, 1,000, 2,000, 3,000

Use the Highest Denominations When Abbreviating Values

For example, never use 1500k (see the x-axis in Chart A in Figure 5.9) (Wong, 2010). There are two solutions: 1) use the highest denomination;

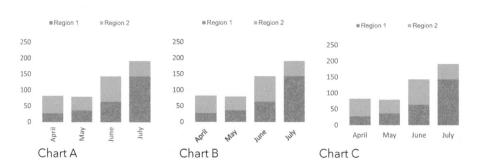

Figure 5.8 Vertical, angled, and horizontal text on the x-axis

Chart A: x-axis abbreviated in thousands

A higher production budget does not necessarily mean more votes.

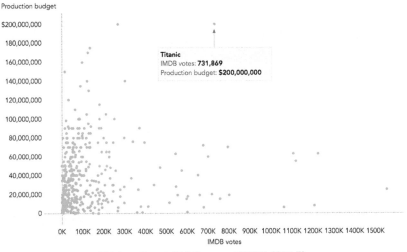

Kristen Sosulski | Source: IMDB (2015)

Chart B: x-axis without abbreviations in thousands

A higher production budget does not necessarily mean more votes

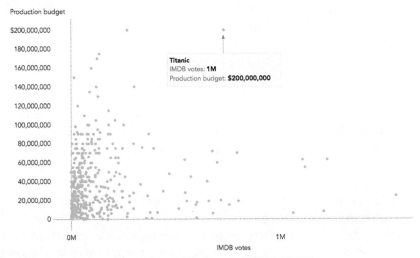

Kristen Sosulski | Source: IMDB (2015)

Figure 5.9 (Continued)

Chart C: x-axis without abbreviated numbers

A higher production budget does not necessarily mean more votes.

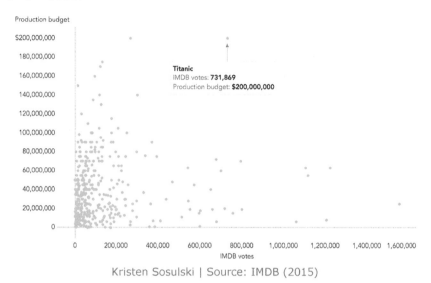

Kristen Sosulski | Source: IMDB (2015)

Figure 5.9 Chart A shows the x-axis scaled in thousands. Chart B shows the x-axis scaled in millions. Chart C shows the scaling without abbreviations.

here, that would be millions rather than thousands; 2) or, do not abbreviate—use the full range of 0 to 1,600,000. However, in this case, as shown in Chart B, using millions would obscure the data; therefore, no abbreviations are used in Chart C.

Keep the maximum value of the y-axis equal to or just above the highest value in the data set. This will fill the height of the chart area. White space might obscure the variation in the data.

For example, in Figure 5.10, Chart A, the highest value is $156.10. Accordingly, the maximum value for the y-axis is $158. For line charts, the minimum value can be set to a number close to the smallest value in the data set (in Chart A, $146.53). The minimum y-axis value is then set to $140, rather than $0. However, in Chart B, the maximum value for the y-axis is set to $180 and the minimum value is $0. This condenses data values in the chart area.

Stock price is an excellent example for using maximum and minimum values to determine the boundaries of the y-axis. It allows the viewer to see variation. This is possible because stock price is usually within a range of numbers greater than zero. Daily or hourly fluctuation

Chart A: Baseline at $140

Apple's stock performance during May 2017 (in USD)

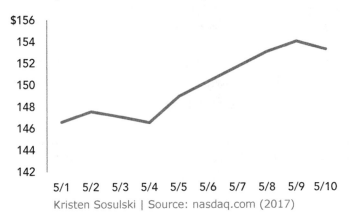

Kristen Sosulski | Source: nasdaq.com (2017)

Chart B: baseline at $0

Apple's stock performance during May 2017 (in USD)

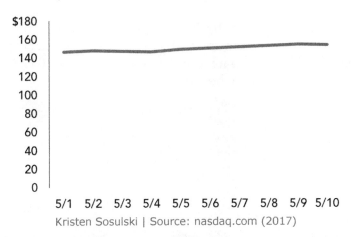

Kristen Sosulski | Source: nasdaq.com (2017)

Figure 5.10 Two charts showing stock price, each with different y-axis scaling

is difficult to discern without a baseline greater than zero. See Chart B, which depicts a relatively flat line.

#6 DATA INTEGRITY

Preserve the integrity of the data as you encode it into a graph. There is a principle, known as the *lie factor*, first articulated by Edward Tufte as: "The representation of numbers, as physically measured on the surface of the graphic itself, should be directly proportional to the quantities represented" (Tufte, 2001 p. 56).

Keep the lie factor equal to 1. Ensure that the size of the effect shown in the graphic equals the size of the effect of the data. The simple formula is:

$$\text{Lie Factor} = \frac{\text{Size effect shown in the graphic (second value-first value)}}{\text{Size effect shown in the data (first value)}}$$

Figure 5.11 is an example a chart with a lie factor greater than 1. The difference in site membership between 2011 and 2012 is:

$$112-106 = 6$$

The size effect shown in the data is:

$$\frac{6}{106} = .056 \ or \ 5.6\%$$

However, the height of the bars inaccurately depicts this percentage change. The difference shown by the graphic can be calculated by measuring the height of each bar. The bar height for 2012 is approximately 4 inches and 1.8 inches for 2011.

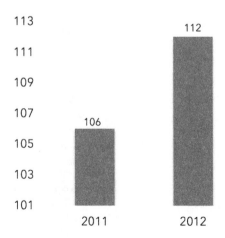

Figure 5.11 An example of a chart with a lie factor greater than 1

The difference in the bar height between 2011 and 2012 is:

$$4 - 1.8 = 2.2$$

The size effect shown by the graphic is:

$$\frac{2.2}{108} = 1.22 \ or \ 122\%$$

Now we can compute the lie factor ratio.

$$\text{Lie Factor} = \frac{\text{Size effect shown in the graphic}}{\text{Size effect shown in the data}} = \frac{1.22}{.056} = 21.78$$

Figure 5.12 presents a comparison of charts with different y-axis minimum starting values. The chart at left over-exaggerates the 5.6% difference by starting the y-axis at 101. To preserve data integrity, the percentage shown in the graphic should conform to the data.

A non-zero baseline is acceptable for some time series charts. For vertical bar charts, use a zero-point y-axis.

Show Your Data Accurately by Avoiding Distortions

For example, 3D graphs show a fake perspective. When I show my students Chart A in Figure 5.13 without the data labels and ask them to report the values for April, their answers are rarely correct. This is by

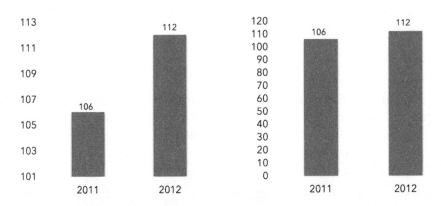

Figure 5.12 A comparison of two charts with different starting y-axis values

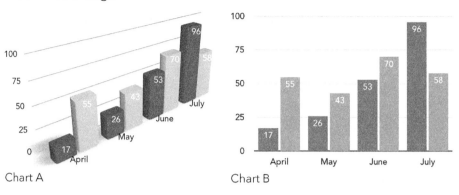

Figure 5.13 A 3D chart compared to a 2D chart

design. It is impossible to accurately determine the height of the vertical bars. This is due to the distortion caused by the 3D perspective. To prove this, I added data labels. The bar labeled with the value of 53 does not even touch the gridline for the y-axis value of 50. Chart B, however, provides the accurate 2D view of the data.

#7 CHARTJUNK

The interior decoration of graphics generates a lot of ink that does not tell the viewer anything new. The purpose of decoration varies—to make the graphic appear more scientific and precise, to enliven the display, to give the designer an opportunity to exercise artistic skills. Regardless of its cause, it is all non–data–ink or redundant data–ink, and it is often chartjunk.

–EDWARD TUFTE, 2001, p. 107

Remove the grid (or use a light gray grid) and non-essential non-data elements. For example, avoid using shadow. Use a white background for your chart, when possible. Decrease non-data graphic elements (e.g., reduce the thickness of the bars in a bar chart). See Table 5.2 for the progression of removing chartjunk from a graph.

See more ways to remove chartjunk from your charts at: http://becomingvisual.com/portfolio/chartjunk

Table 5.2 A graph with chartjunk removed in 10 steps

Original chart	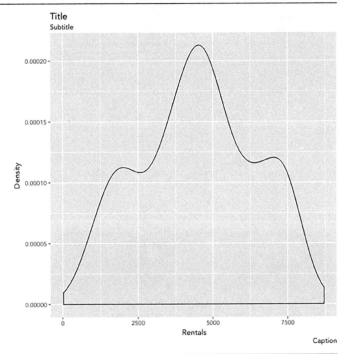
Step 2: Removed gray background, filled the graphic and changed the outline of the density plot from black to the fill color to define the graphic	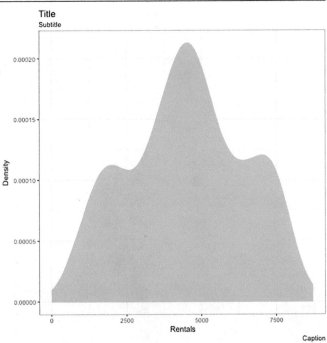

(Continued)

Table 5.2 (Continued)

Step 3: Removed chart border	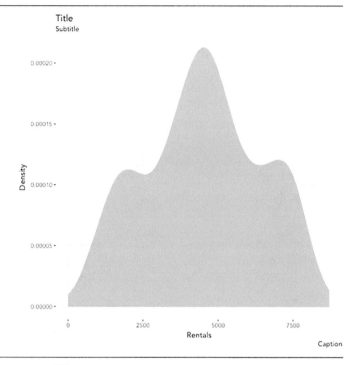
Step 4: Removed major gridlines	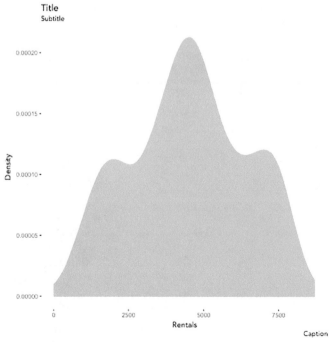

Step 5: Removed minor gridlines

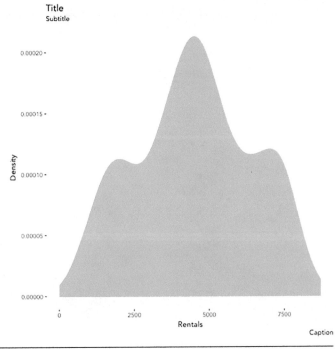

Step 6: Changed the x-axis and y-axis lines to a light gray color (1f)

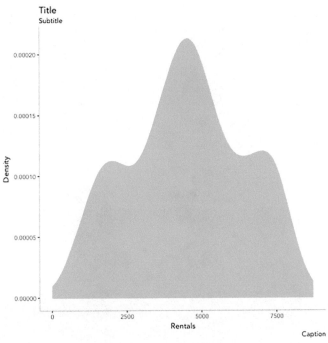

(Continued)

Table 5.2 (Continued)

Step 7: Removed the
x-axis tick marks (1g)

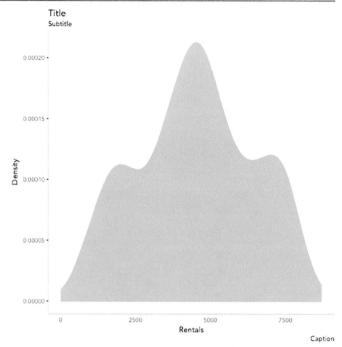

Step 8: Removed the
y-axis tick marks (1h)

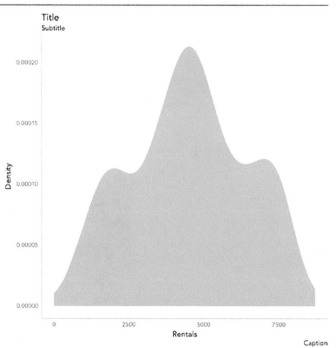

Step 9: Formatted
the x-axis scale with
commas

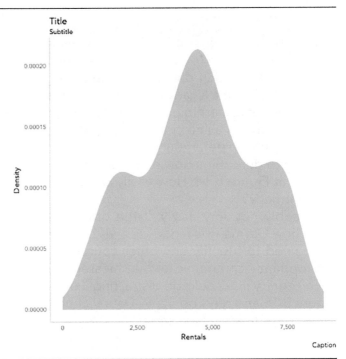

Step 10: Added
a vertical line for
the mean as a
preattentive attribute

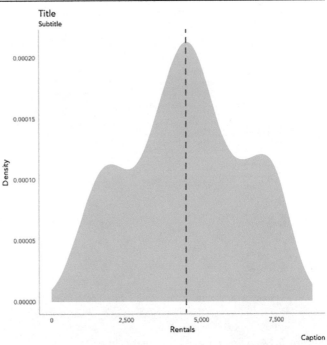

#8 DATA DENSITY

Data density refers to the amount of data shown in a visualization through encodings (points, bars, lines, etc.). A common mistake is presenting too much data in a single data graph. The data itself can obscure the insight. It can make the chart unreadable because the data values are not discernible. Examples include: overlapping data points, too many lines in a line chart, or too many slices in a pie chart. Selecting the appropriate amount of data requires a delicate balance. It is your job to determine how much detail is necessary.

Look at Figure 5.14. How easily can you locate Brazil and compare it to Germany?

Probably not very easily. If the other line series are there just to show how Germany is faring vis-a-vis other top economies, then there is no need to identify any other country by name. This chart would appropriately communicate that message. Using a different color for each country line could be distracting. Look at the approach shown in Figure 5.15 and read point #9–Data Richness for an alternative way of presenting multiple time series.

The changing population growth of the world's top economies

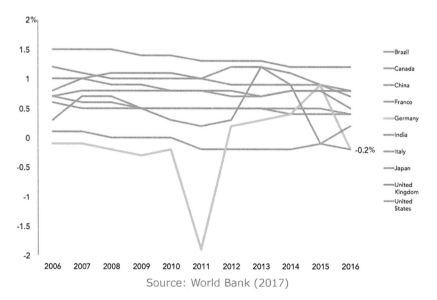

Source: World Bank (2017)

Figure 5.14 A line chart with 10 data series

The changing population growth of the world's top economies shows Germany and Japan on the decline in 2016.

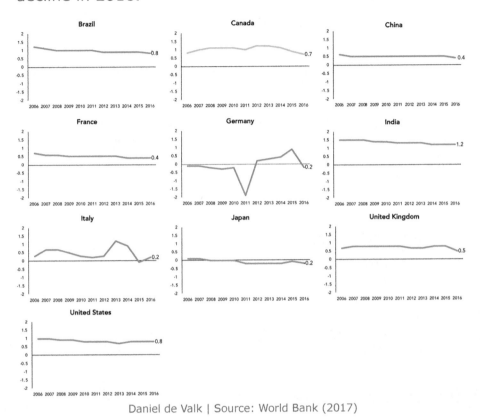

Daniel de Valk | Source: World Bank (2017)

Figure 5.15 A small multiple display of 10 line charts

#9 DATA RICHNESS

High-quality data is data that come from reputable sources and are accurate. Data richness refers to the quality of the data and how much data must be shown to provide an accurate picture. In terms of data richness—if it is important to know which line represented which country—each line would need to be 1) labeled with the country name; or 2) represented by a different color. For a line chart with more than four series, both options make distinguishing the lines difficult.

Rework the chart presented in Figure 5.14. Modify the chart to label each line. Then create another chart and use a different color line for each country. Evaluate which chart shows the data best. Download the example from http://becoming visual.com/portfolio/datarichness

An alternative way of presenting multiple time series is to create a matrix of charts. Tufte (2001 has coined the term *small multiples* to describe this type of chart presentation. Figure 5.15 shows a snapshot of each country and the population growth over the past decade with one small chart for each country. Keep the x-axis and y-axis values the same for all small multiples. This ensures equal comparison among charts. This also solves the data density issue. This is a useful way of comparing variables to one another.

#10 ATTRIBUTION

Always include a citation to the source of the data in your visualizations. Include the year the data set was created. Also, give yourself credit for creating the chart.

Your Name | Data Source: data.com (Year)

Now, return to Figure 5.9. Note the attribution in the lower right-hand corner of the chart. Find a format that works for you.

Interview with a practitioner

I interviewed Jake Curtis from Return Path who described how he uses data graphics in his practice. See the full color version at: http://becomingvisual.com/portfolio/returnpath

Kristen Sosulski (KS)   **Jake Curtis (JC)**

KS:

Who are you and what do you do?

JC:

My name is Jake Curtis. I work on the Innovation Labs team where our mission is to test and launch new products quickly; we are largely focused on finding new ways to use our vast data resources to build solutions for our email marketing customers.

Return Path is the industry expert in email deliverability, which is the way email marketers measure the success at which their email campaigns reach subscribers' inboxes. Our SaaS offering provides insights that allow for quick discovery of inbox placement issues with corrective action to improve deliverability. Powering our solutions is the Return Path Data Exchange, the world's most comprehensive source of data from the email ecosystem, including 70+ mailbox and security provider partners, covering 2.5 billion inboxes–approximately 70% of the worldwide total. On top of that, we've built the Return Path Consumer Network of two million+ consumers, which allows us to gather insights into user behavior, brand affinity, and consumer preferences through how they interact with their email inboxes.

In my role as Sales Enablement Manager, I am tasked with developing how we communicate the value of our solutions with clients, including managing beta clients to test our solutions, gathering feedback throughout the process and continuously iterating product positioning, and sharing feedback with Product Management.

KS:

How do you use data visualization in your practice?

JC:

I'm currently working on a product that provides automated recommendations to improve deliverability for our email marketers' clients. For example, Gmail is notoriously difficult because of the sophisticated algorithms they use to determine where to place messages for its users, whether the Inbox (and which tab) or Spam folder. Most notably, they focus on individual users' relative engagement–how they engage with email from a particular domain versus other messages in their inbox overall. So, to deliver your email successfully at Gmail, you want your subscribers to open and click your messages to ensure continued inbox folder placement. If too many subscribers do not engage, it is likely many of your messages may end up in the Spam folder, negatively impacting email engagement and resulting conversions from that marketing channel. Most other mailbox providers like Yahoo! and AOL don't have this kind of nuance to deliverability at the individual user level.

To communicate the impact of our product, the before and after, we need to demonstrate that our clients have suboptimal deliverability at a particular mailbox provider, convince them to take action by using our product, and then illustrate our results. Data visualization is a vital component to telling this story because this product addresses a very niche problem and we need to clearly communicate its value.

KS:

Can you share an example of how you have used data visualization in your practice? (show data graphic itself). What insight is evidenced by the graph provided? What did you do with that insight? (make a decision, inform policy, predict the future, etc.)

JC:

I joined a small team of engineers, data scientists, a UX designer and a product manager and came into it in a later stage when we wanted to test it with customers. We built an internal tool to plot inbox placement by domain, but it was not intuitive for clients. My challenge was how to show a client who may know little about email deliverability why inbox placement is important. Here's what I had to work with initially:

Daily Inbox Rates by Engagement Group

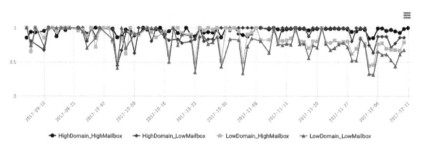

Daily Inbox Rates by Engagement Group

Active Subscribers

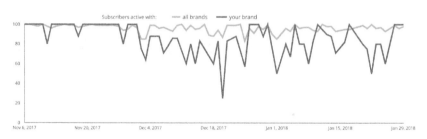

Less-active Subscribers

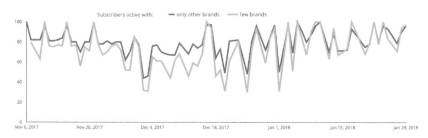

I have very talented UX designer colleagues who were focused on larger projects such as how this product fits in the client workflow and did not have the bandwidth to focus on this particular chart. And because I was having issues explaining the data to clients and they were not understanding it, I took it upon myself to revise it and later consulted with them for final adjustments. Here's what I came up with:

These two charts show inbox placement (as a percent) on the x-axis over time, measured from subscribers who receive email from a particular domain. The first chart shows two lines that represent two different groups of active subscribers.

Subscribers that are active with "all brands" (green line) interact with email from this domain and other domains in their inbox at a high rate. Subscribers that are active with "your brand" (grey line) interact with email from this domain at a *higher* rate than other domains in their inbox.

The second chart is similar but for less-active subscribers. Subscribers that are active with "only other brands" (black line) are *less* active with this domain compared to other domains in their inbox. Subscribers that are active with "few brands" (green line) are less active with both *this* domain and other domains in their inbox.

This helps illustrate to a client that inbox placement may be different for different groups of their subscribers and that the solution I am proposing can help improve this issue, by keeping inbox placement consistently high for active subscribers and increase and reduce the variance for less-active subscribers.

KS:

How did you create it? What was that data? What was the software? What would have been the alternative?

JC:

I recently learned how to use Tableau for a class, but my license expired and I could not justify a corporate license. So instead I used Google Data Studio which came bundled with G Suite. At first, I found it almost confusingly simple compared to Tableau but quickly got the hang of it. The first things I considered—what was I struggling to explain using the original chart and what questions were my clients asking? That led me to creating two charts with each having its own story and similarities. From there I scrutinized every detail and asked if it added anything to the story or detracted from it because it was an unnecessary embellishment. It was hard to think of an alternative to a line chart because the data is a time series. I did consider a scatterplot but concluded it was important to visualize trends by date so the customer can relate back to a particular campaign. Finally, line charts are common in email marketing, and I wanted to keep it relatable to the client.

The 10 design standards presented in this chapter are non-trivial to implement. The standards entail developing a literacy in how to use and alter charts using formatting features of the software. In addition, applying the standards consistently, as part of your practice, requires diligence and patience. Developing the requisite skills to alter your data graphics to adhere to the design standards moves you one step closer to presenting the data clearly and allowing it to present itself over the other graphical, non-data elements.

The checklist below is a handy reminder of the 10 design standards. Share the checklist with colleagues and use it to inform the design of your visualizations.

5.2 Design Standards Checklist

TEN DESIGN STANDARDS FOR CHARTS AND GRAPHS

☐ Chart format: select the appropriate chart format for your data and audience. Decide whether the chart will be printed, projected, or used on the web.

☐ Color: use color sparingly. Use it to highlight a data point as a pre-attentive attribute. Consider using grayscale shading rather than color. Avoid thematic or decorative presentations. Consider the cultural meanings of the colors you select and the impact that may have on your audience. Ensure high contrast values. Test contrast by converting colors to grayscale.

☐ Text and labels: use descriptive text and labels. For small series bar and line charts, remove the y-axis and place value labels directly on the data encodings. Use a legend when the chart encodings are too small to label and/or if they would impede readability. Add a description to guide readers in interpreting your visualization.

☐ Readability: font face, size, direction, and color affect the legibility. Do not set text at an angle or vertically.

☐ Scales: keep the maximum value of the y-axis equal to or just above the highest value in the data set. Ensure a zero-point y-axis for vertical bar charts. Use natural increments for scales.

☐ Data integrity: show your data accurately and avoid distortions. Avoid fake perspectives, such as 3D. Keep the lie factor equal to 1. Ensure that the size of the effect shown in the graphic equals the size of the effect of the data.

☐ Chartjunk (Tufte, 2001): remove the grid (or use a light gray grid) and non-essential elements. Avoid using shadows. Stick to white or match the chart background. Emphasize the data and reduce the non-data graphic elements.
☐ Data density: consider how much information is shown in a graphic. Use small multiples to show comparisons of multivariate data.
☐ Data richness: accurate data and effective filtering of your data.
☐ Attribution: provide a citation. Include year for data used and add a chart author.

5.3 Exercises

EXERCISE 1. CRITIQUE

The critique and analysis of data visualizations allow designers to practice applying these principles. The standards presented in this chapter provide a concrete set of criteria you can use to evaluate visualizations.

The chart in Figure 5.16 shows the unemployment rate over time. Your task is to identify those design practices that obscure the data and those that elucidate the data. Use the table below to indicate

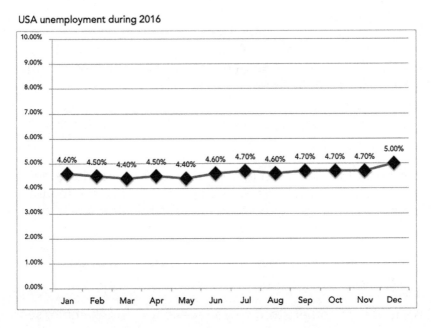

Figure 5.16 A line chart for critique

which design aesthetics support or hinder your understanding of the visual information.

Design principle	Support	Hinder
Chart format		
Color		
Text and labels		
Readability		
Scales		
Data integrity		
Chartjunk		
Data density		
Data richness		
Attribution		

EXERCISE 2. APPLICATION OF RECOMMENDATIONS FROM YOUR CRITIQUE

Next, recreate the chart. Begin reviewing the data to see how it is organized. Download the data file at http://becomingvisual.com/usa_unemployment_2016.csv

Select the data and visual display option that best conveys the desired message. Then, refine your display; apply the principles of design to show the data clearly. Be sure you have identified and high-lighted a key insight to show.

EXERCISE 3. INCORPORATING FEEDBACK INTO YOUR PRACTICE

Sharing is a dominant theme in this book. Once you have designed and refined your visualizations, the next step is to seek feedback on your visualizations. Ask others to identify the key insight or answer spe-cific questions such as

"True or false? From 2002 to 2012, Jamaica's rural population did not grow."

Make it easy for others to give you feedback. For example, send an email with the visualization to a colleague. Ask for a simple response to a question, such as True or False. You can also create a Google Form to collect the feedback and make it anonymous.

Ultimately, you want others to glean the right insight from your visualization. Therefore, it's important to ask them for feedback.

Note

1 Amazon's online market place for work.

Bibliography

Bureau of Labor Statistics. (2017). Labor force statistics from the current population survey. Retrieved from https://data.bls.gov/timeseries/LNS14000000

Few, S. (2012). *Show me the numbers: Designing tables and graphs to enlighten*. Burlingame, CA: Analytics Press.

Nasdaq. Apple Inc. common stock quote and summary data. Retrieved from www.nasdaq.com/symbol/aapl on June 1, 2017

Tufte, E. R. (1997). *Visual explanations: Images and quantities, evidence and narrative*. Cheshire, CT: Graphics Press. Retrieved from http://catalog.hathitrust.org/Record/003159488

Tufte, E. R. (2001). *The visual display of quantitative information*. Cheshire, CT: Graphics Press.

Wong, D. M. (2010). *The Wall Street Journal guide to information graphics: The dos and don'ts of presenting data, facts, and figures*. New York, NY: W. W. Norton & Company.

The World Bank. (2017). World development indicators. Retrieved from http://databank.worldbank.org/data/reports.aspx?source=world-development-indicators&preview=on on September 15, 2017

VI

THE
AUDIENCE

How do you optimize your data story for your audience?

Good data visualizations are persuasive graphics that help tell your data story. When you begin any visualization project, how do you know if your audience will understand your message? Your audience has input in the data visualization process. Consider what they already know and don't know. Determine how you will support them in identifying and understanding your key points.

To begin, think about the basic information that you need to communicate through every data graphic.

Five questions guide your explanations of data graphics:

1. **What do the data axes mean?**

   Upon showing the data graphic, orient your audience by explaining the x- and y-axes (for Cartesian plots), the geographical scale (for maps), and the nodes and edges (for network diagrams).

   To explain the axes in the chart above, your description could read as follows:

   We are looking at a stacked area chart that shows the years (2012 through 2016) on the x-axis, and the gross domestic product (GDP) by country, for four countries, in U.S. dollars, plotted on the y-axis.

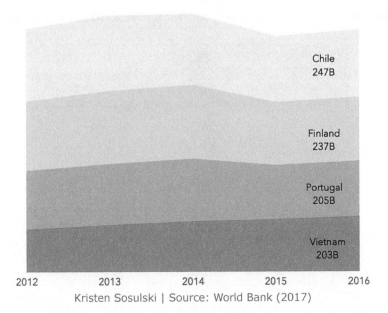

Kristen Sosulski | Source: World Bank (2017)

2. **What do the encodings mean (the value of the data points)?**

This requires an explanation of the meaning of the circles, bubbles, bars, points, shaded regions, lines, and/or colors.

Example: each country is represented by a different shade of gray. Each country's gross domestic product (the total value of everything produced by its people and companies), for each year (2012 through 2016) is labeled.

3. **What level of detail is presented?**

The level of detail refers to the way the data is aggregated or summarized—for instance, data such as bicycle rentals can be viewed at the yearly, monthly, daily, or hourly level of detail.

Example: we are only looking at the change in GDP growth for four out of 217 economies in the world. These countries rank between 42 and 46 out of 217 economies. Chile is currently ranked 42, Finland is 43, Portugal is 45 and Vietnam is 46.

4. **What data points should they be looking at?**

Draw your audience's attention to the most important part of the chart. Show the trend, pattern, anomaly, etc. that is critical to your message. This may involve highlighting a data series or building the data series incrementally (see the chart below).

Example: in green, I have added two other data series. The revenue of Walmart and Exxon Mobil. Exxon's revenue is larger than

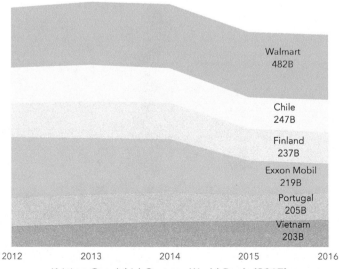

Kristen Sosulski | Source: World Bank (2017)

that of Portugal (the 45th largest economy in the world). Walmart's revenue is more than twice as large as Finland's, Portugal's, Vietnam's, and larger than 194 other economies.

5. **What is the key takeaway by my audience from the chart(s)?**

   Leave your audience with a question to prompt discussion, a result, conclusion, or finding for each chart.

   Example: if Walmart's revenue was GDP, it would be the 23rd largest economy in the world, just behind Sweden. When we compare Measuring dollar-value GDP against dollar-value firm revenue, we realize the vast power corporations hold, which raises interesting questions. Do corporations have obligations to civil society? How can corporations be held accountable?[1]"

If you can answer these five questions for your data graphics, then you can ensure you are using your graphics with purpose.

6.1 Optimize Your Data Story

There may be times when you don't know who the ultimate audience will be for your data story. At the most fundamental level, you have to design data graphics that make your key message obvious. You will need to take into account how human beings process information to optimize your data story for them. There are two simple ways to optimize your data story.

MINIMIZE INFORMATION OVERLOAD

Deconstruct every presentation into three components: words, images, and sound (if there is narration accompanying the visualization). Human beings have separate channels for processing visual and auditory information. However, our processing capacity is limited because our visual and auditory channels can only handle a certain amount of information at one time. The key in presentations is not to overwhelm a single channel, which could result in information overload.

You don't need to be a cognitive psychologist to recognize information overload. Think about the last presentation you attended. Did the presenter read off his or her slides? Did the information presented on the slides support the speaker or replicate what the speaker was saying? Did the speaker go overtime or have too many slides for the time given? Was there no time for questions because the presenter spoke too long? If you answered yes to any of these questions, it's possible that you experienced information overload. Be considerate of your audience. Design your presentation to fit within the allotted time frame and allow time for discussion.

MAXIMIZE RETENTION

A trick that I learned early on in my career was to treat every presentation as if I was trying to teach the audience something. Retention and learning go hand in hand. If you want the audience to remember something, they need to engage in active learning.

Humans engage in active learning by attending to relevant incoming information, organizing selected information into coherent mental representations, and integrating mental representations with other knowledge.
–RICHARD MAYER, 2001, p. 103

Figure 6.1 illustrates the pathway of incoming information through the human information processing system.[2] Our processing systems comprise three memory stores: sensory memory, working memory, and long-term memory. The objective is to present information that is learned and, ultimately, stored in long-term memory. Basically, you want people to remember what you say and show.

The first stage of the model is the sensory memory. As images and spoken words are presented, they enter sensory memory through our eyes and ears. Sensory memory allows for pictures and text to be held in visual sensory memory as exact visual images for a very brief time period.

Working memory is used for temporarily holding storage. For example, when your audience is listening and viewing a live presentation with sounds, images, and written words, some of that information will

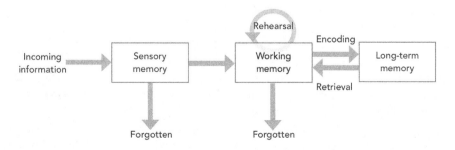

Figure 6.1 The human information processing system

become incorporated into mental representations of the knowledge. Then, the information will move from working memory to long-term memory. This involves incorporating the new information into a body of existing knowledge. Can you aid in connecting the new information with information your audience knows? Can you provide opportunities to put the new knowledge represented into practice? For example, practice or rehearsal of information can done through a discussion or activity. The objective is to integrate the new knowledge into long-term memory where knowledge schemas are altered.

6.2 Strategies for Maximizing Retention and Minimizing Overload

Use these four strategies to maximize retention and reduce information overload:

1. Design visual information that is easily perceived.
2. Reinforce the message.
3. Build on prior knowledge to integrate new knowledge.
4. Show displays the audience can interpret.

1. DESIGN VISUAL INFORMATION THAT IS EASILY PERCEIVED

How can you design to ensure incoming visual information will be easily perceived?

For audiences to process information, it must have their attention. Therefore, designers must optimize visual content for sensory memory. To focus on the important information, some other information must be filtered out. For example, if you are in a meeting and you hear a horn honking outside, you may filter it out.

Along the same lines, if you were shown the graphic in Figure 6.2, what would catch your attention?

What stands out may be different for each of us. In this chart, no single attribute is featured more prominently than another. The lines and data symbols may seem confusing and hard to follow. Most importantly, you may not know what the key insight is or where to focus. Now, look at Figure 6.3. Notice that the attributes are made clear through highlighting a single series (in green) and adding a value label (32K). In addition, the triangle data symbols are removed and the other series

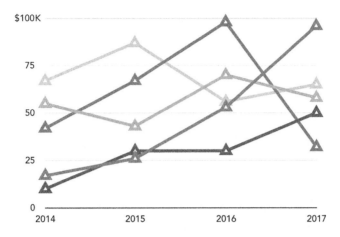

Figure 6.2 A line chart showing five time series of gross sales by product over a four-year period

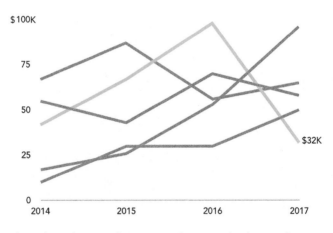

Figure 6.3 A line chart showing five series of gross sales by product over a four-year period with one product highlighted

are shaded the same color. These enhancements are intended to capture the viewer's attention. This illustrates the use of preattentive attributes. These attributes are shapes, colors, positions, and movements that are seen immediately.

Typically, tasks that can be performed on large multi-element displays in less than 200 to 250 milliseconds (msec) are considered preattentive.
                        –CHRISTOPHER G. HEALEY, 2012, p. 2

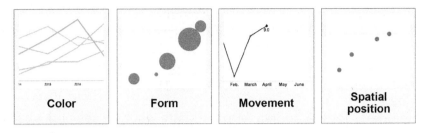

Figure 6.4 Preattentive attributes for use in data visualizations

Colin Ware (2013), in *Information Visualization: Perception for Design*, defines four preattentive visual properties. These include color, form, movement, and spatial position (see Figure 6.4).

As you design your data visualizations, use the above easily perceived attributes to direct your audience's attention to the most important details. For example, use a contrasting color to highlight a single series or data point that is important to your message. Selecting a chart type that clearly shows differences in form, such as the length of bars or size of bubbles, is useful for comparisons. Movement or animation works well for showing time series data slowly, one data point at a time. This technique is useful when the presenter is talking the audience through a chart. Finally, spatial position is a preattentive attribute in which your visualized data reveals outliers, clusters, or trends that are easily seen.

2. REINFORCE THE MESSAGE

Now that we have discussed strategies to help your audience recognize and process the right visual information, how will they process the right words or oral information?

There are three types of explanations that can accompany a chart. How do you decide on one?

- *Oral presentation*. Use spoken words to describe what the audience is seeing.
- *Oral static narration*. For video-based/recorded presentations, oral narration guides the viewer in a way similar to a live presentation. There is no interaction with the audience.

- *Written explanations.* Written communication for chart titles, descriptions. Essentially, anything you want the audience to read.

Words help reinforce a message. For live presentations, the words spoken should differ from those written to avoid information overload.

The goal is for the audience to integrate what we say and what we show into their prior knowledge in order to commit the information to long-term memory. Techniques that may help for images that contain written and spoken words include the following.

Present the Data Graphic and the Related Words Near Each Other

We learn better when corresponding words and pictures are presented near rather than far from each other.
    –RICHARD MAYER, 2001, p. 110

For example, Figure 6.5 presents the values for the bars using the scale on the y-axis. This requires reading the y-axis to see the value of each bar. However, Figure 6.6 labels the bars directly and provides a title right above the chart.

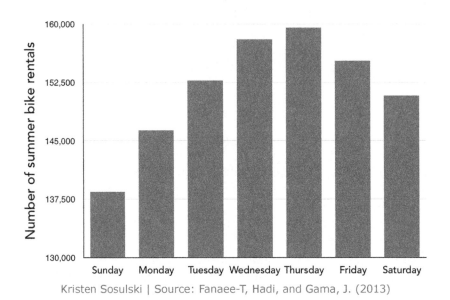

Kristen Sosulski | Source: Fanaee-T, Hadi, and Gama, J. (2013)

Figure 6.5 A bar chart showing bike rentals by day with the data values presented on the y-axis

Summer bicycle rentals by day

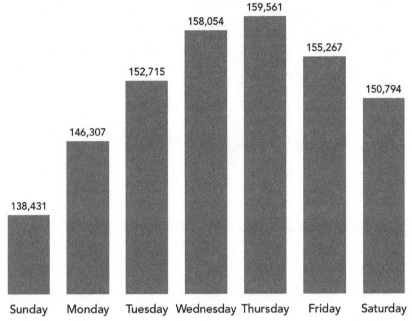

Kristen Sosulski | Source: Fanaee-T, Hadi, and Gama, J. (2013)

Figure 6.6 A bar chart showing bike rentals by day with the data labels directly on top of the bars and the y-axis scale removed

Avoid Using Irrelevant Words and Pictures

Only use charts that add to your message. For example, if the message is that the most popular day for renting bikes in the summer is Thursday, it would make sense to show that insight by comparing it to other days of the week. It would not be useful to show the total rentals for all seasons by day of the week (as shown in Figure 6.7). The number of rentals by day is difficult to decipher. Rather, showing rentals by day over a the summer provides the visual evidence to support your point (see Figure 6.6).

In addition, words should be read or heard—not both. Decide which one supports the key takeaway for your audience.

For example, to present the key takeaway that the most popular day for renting bikes is Thursday, you can easily highlight the bar (for Thursday), and orally explain the key takeaway vis-a-vis the other days of the week (see Figure 6.8).

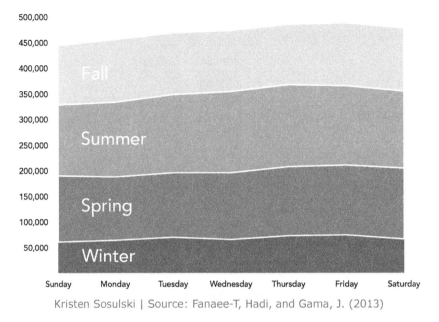

Figure 6.7 A chart that obscures the key takeaway in the data

Summer bicycle rentals by day

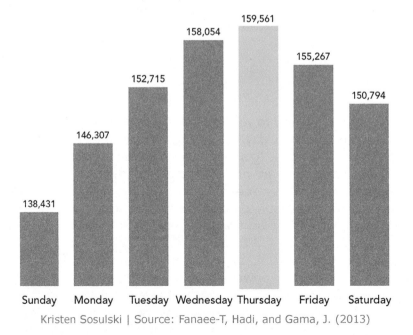

Figure 6.8 A vertical bar chart that shows the key takeaway presented in the data graphic highlighted in green

Thursday is the most popular day for rentals in the summer.

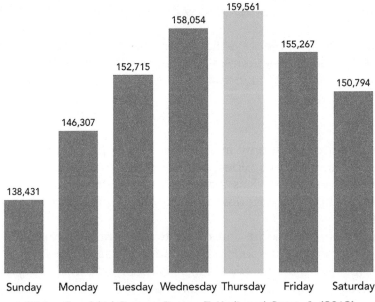

Kristen Sosulski | Source: Fanaee-T, Hadi, and Gama, J. (2013)

Figure 6.9 A vertical bar chart that shows the key takeaway presented in the data graphic highlighted in green along with explanatory text

Otherwise, provide some explanatory text that can be displayed for the audience to read. Do not read the text to the audience. See Figure 6.9.

Redundant text and narration hinder your message, rather than reinforce it (Mayer, 2001).

 ## 3. Build on Prior Knowledge to Integrate New Knowledge

Building on the prior knowledge of your audience can foster understanding. Ask yourself, what does my audience already know about the topic? What don't they yet know?

For example, if I were to deliver a presentation on different types of charts used to visualize data, I would want to know how much my audience knows about the topic. Specifically, I would be careful not to waste my audience's time by speaking to topics that they know very well. Rather, I would build on their knowledge in order to introduce them to something new but related to what they already know.

There are two simple ways that I could determine what they already know. 1) I could survey them in advance, or 2) I could ask them questions during the presentation.

The Survey

I could send out a survey in advance to the participants. The survey would contain two types of questions: content questions and perception questions. This approach allows the audience to rate knowledge through a series of perception questions as shown in Figure 6.10.

In addition, by asking one or more content questions (see Figure 6.11), I can assess specific knowledge areas of my audience.

After reviewing the survey results, I can begin to design my content at the level appropriate for my audience.

Rate your skill level with the following technologies:

	No knowledge	Very Poor	Poor	Average	Good	Very Good
Excel	○	○	○	○	○	○
Tableau	○	○	○	○	○	○
Adobe Photoshop	○	○	○	○	○	○
PowerPoint	○	○	○	○	○	○
Google Charts	○	○	○	○	○	○
JavaScript	○	○	○	○	○	○
HTML	○	○	○	○	○	○
CSS	○	○	○	○	○	○
R	○	○	○	○	○	○
Python	○	○	○	○	○	○

Figure 6.10 A survey that asks the user to rate their skills

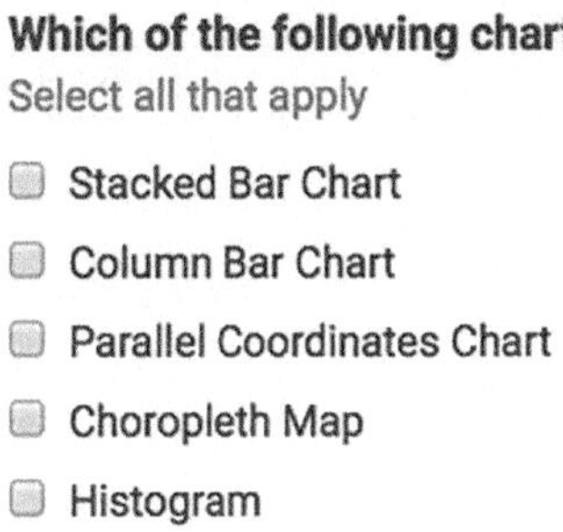

Which of the following charts could you use to show categorical data?

Select all that apply

☐ Stacked Bar Chart

☐ Column Bar Chart

☐ Parallel Coordinates Chart

☐ Choropleth Map

☐ Histogram

Figure 6.11 An example of a content question used to assess knowledge

Design decisions must be made up front in terms of the level of prior knowledge necessary to understand the visualized information. The prior knowledge problem can be seen as a need for adaptive information visualization systems in response to accumulated knowledge of their users.

–CHAOMEN CHEN, 2005, para. 16

For example, if I knew everyone in the audience was familiar with working with categorical data, but less familiar with working with time series data, I could build on their prior knowledge. Specifically, I would speak to the audience about what they know about categorical data. Then, I would introduce a time series element to the categorical data as a way to extend their understanding. The example shown in Table 6.1 is an example of categorical data collected from a survey. Each column represents a question related to the level of proficiency in a particular software program. Table 6.2 shows that same data with an added column: *Timestamp*. The timestamp adds a time element to the data that shows when the surveys were submitted. Finally, I could show how timestamp data can be visualized using a line chart (see Figure 6.12).

After accessing my audience's existing understanding of categorical data, I can introduce time series data by showing how categorical data can have a time series element. The audience can expand their view of data by comparing and contrasting the difference in the columns of categorical versus time series data.

Table 6.1 A snapshot of categorical data collected from a survey

Excel	Tableau	Photoshop
Good	Very Good	No knowledge
Good	Good	Good
Very Good	Average	No Knowledge
Very Good	Very Good	Poor
Average	Poor	No Knowledge
Very Good	Poor	No Knowledge
Good	Poor	No Knowledge
Good	Poor	Poor
Good	Poor	Poor

Table 6.2 A snapshot of categorical and time series data collected from a survey

Timestamp	Excel	Tableau	Photoshop
9/19/2016 18:07	Good	Very Good	No knowledge
9/19/2016 18:34	Good	Good	Good
9/19/2016 19:41	Very Good	Average	No Knowledge
9/19/2016 20:49	Very Good	Very Good	Poor
9/19/2016 21:37	Average	Poor	No Knowledge
9/20/2016 6:28	Very Good	Poor	No Knowledge
9/20/2016 18:59	Good	Poor	No Knowledge
9/20/2016 14:50	Good	Poor	Poor
9/20/2016 17:46	Good	Poor	Poor

Number of daily responses

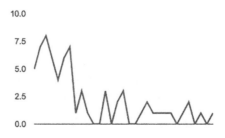

Figure 6.12 A line chart of the time stamp data from the survey

Ask Questions During the Presentation

Consider asking the audience a few questions that would allow you to build on their prior knowledge. A series of questions and answers engages an audience. Prepare for the range of responses to the questions and adjust the nature of your presentation from there.

If you are unable to survey your audience or ask them questions during the presentation, you can do some research on your own. For example, if your audience is filled with colleagues in your profession, you may have insight into what they do and don't know about the subject. You can solicit feedback in advance from a few colleagues by asking them to review your charts. Some basic questions you can ask include:

- Are the text and labels easy to read?
- What is the key takeaway from the chart?
- Is there anything that is unclear?

Then, use the feedback to revise your charts.

Using surveys, asking for feedback from colleagues, and interacting with your audience are just a few ways to understand the prior knowledge of your audience. Once you have an understanding of their prior knowledge, you can build upon it to engage them and introduce the new ideas or concepts.

4. SHOW DISPLAYS THAT THE AUDIENCE CAN INTERPRET

Has your audience seen this chart type before?

Visual literacy is an important aspect of prior knowledge. Is the display type you are showing in line with other charts or graphs they have seen in the past?

For example, if your audience is familiar with line charts for comparing time series data and you show them a radar chart, they may not know how to read it or derive meaning from it. Look at the radar chart in Figure 6.13. Compare it to the line chart in Figure 6.14. Each chart uses lines to represent the time series for casual riders, registered users, and total rentals over the 94 days of summer. However, the radar chart makes it more difficult to compare the values across each variable.

Radar Chart	Line Chart
It is more difficult to compare variables because they could each have independent scales.	Comparing variables is easy because they all share a common axis and scales.
It's too easy to only look at the size and compare the area.	The direction of the line tells you the performance of the variable.

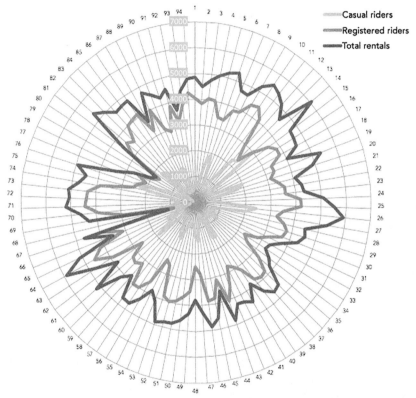

Kristen Sosulski | Source: Fanaee-T, Hadi, and Gama, J. (2013)

Figure 6.13 A radar chart of bike rentals per day in the summer

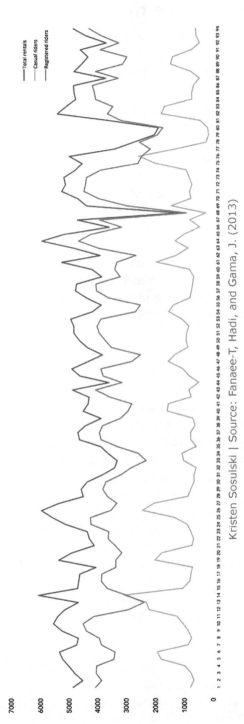

Figure 6.14 A time series line chart of bike rentals per day in the summer

Kristen Sosulski | Source: Fanaee-T, Hadi, and Gama, J. (2013)

6.3 Communicate the Key Message

Now that you have optimized your data graphics, assist your audience in identifying the key message. The audience should not struggle to decipher the key message of your visualizations. This means that your data insights must shine through the displays you create.

You want your audience to remember your key takeaway. The takeaway can be defined as the key insight you would like your audience to remember. For example, are you trying to alter their beliefs? Are you trying to persuade them? Provide them with some key facts? Why should they care about what you have to say? This requires you to switch your perspective and put yourself in the shoes of the audience. Consider their motivation for engaging with your content. Seek to ensure understanding by finding ways to solicit feedback, input, or dialogue from your audience.

While it is not always possible to have an interactive experience with the audience, consider how to maximize their understanding through good chart design. Design aesthetics play a large part in keeping the visualization simple and interpretable. Results presented should be clear, not cryptic.

6.4 Exercises

1. Build three charts (using any visualization tool).
   a. Audience: survey respondents that completed the survey shown in Figure 6.10.
   b. Data: download the sample survey data about users and their technical skill set as it relates to data visualization at: http:// becomingvisual.com/ surveydata.csv
   c. Insight: explore the data to find an insight worth sharing through a visualization related to the skill set of the respondents.
   d. Display: create three different displays that show the skill set of the sample respondents: A vertical bar chart, radar chart, and stacked bar chart.
2. How would you use preattentive attributes in the charts you created in exercise 1? Add one to each chart.

Notes

1 (Global Policy Forum, 2017, para 1)
2 The model in Figure 6.1 was originally proposed by Richard Atkinson and Richard Shiffrin in 1968. It only contained the working memory and long-term memory stores. The Atkinson–Shiffrin model has since evolved to include a sensory memory.

Bibliography

Chen, C. (2005). Top 10 unsolved information visualization problems. *IEEE Computer Graphics and Applications, 25*(4). Retrieved from http://ieeexplore.ieee.org/document/1463074/

Fanaee-T, H., & Gama, J. (2014). Event labeling combining ensemble detectors and background knowledge. *Progress in Artificial Intelligence, 2*(2), 1–15. doi:10.1007/s13748-013-0040-3

Global Policy Forum. (2017). Comparison of the world's 25 largest corporations with the GDP of selected countries. Retrieved from www.globalpolicy.org/component/content/article/150-general/50950-comparison-of-the-worlds-25-largest-corporations-with-the-gdp-of-selected-countries.html

Healey, C. G., & Enns, J. T. (2012). Attention and visual memory in visualization and computer graphics. *IEEE Transactions on Visualization and Computer Graphics, 18*(7), 1170–1188.

Mayer, R. E. (2001). *Multimedia learning*. Cambridge: Cambridge University Press.

Ware, C. (2013). *Information visualization: Perception for design* (3rd ed.). Burlington, MA: Morgan Kaufmann.

VII

THE
PRESENTATION

What is the best way to use data graphics in a presentation?

Think about the last great presentation you attended? Was the presenter engaging? How did the presenter use slides? What do you remember from the presentation?

We have all been in situations where we have to sit through a poor presentation. The slides were difficult to read for one reason or another. Maybe the information presented was overwhelming, or worse, it was just plain boring.

Look at the slide in Figure 7.1. What do you think the speaker is doing while this slide is projected on the screen? Is he or she reading the text from the slide? Explaining the key insight from the chart? Now, imagine yourself in the audience. What would you be doing as this slide was projected? Would you be trying to decipher the chart, read the text, or both? This is an example of a poorly designed slide. How can it be improved? Take a moment to write down how you would revise this slide (before turning the page).

Here are a few things that can be corrected.

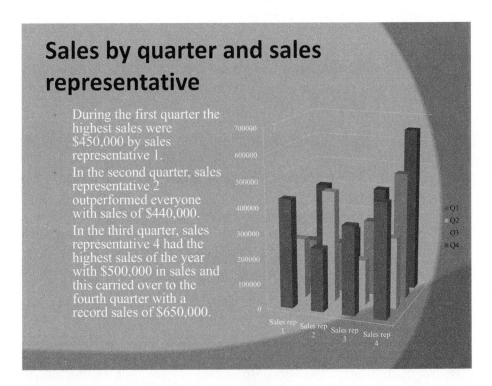

Figure 7.1 A sample slide used in a live presentation

1. Slide background color

    The dark gray three-toned slide background makes both black text and white text difficult to read. Backgrounds should be kept simple with only one shade, such as black or white.

2. Font face, size, and color

    The font face is Times New Roman, a font usually used for printed text. For text presented on a screen, a sans-serif font, such as Verdana, Arial, Avenir, or Helvetica, tends to be easier to read (Michael Bernard, Lida, Riley, Hackler, & Janzen, 2002). The font size of the chart labels is 12-point. This size works nicely for printed documents, but text for projected slides should be at least 16-point. Also, there is too much text on the slide. The text color should offer a high contrast to the background. Both the white text and black text are difficult to read in this slide.

    What if the speaker just showed the chart and eliminated the text all together? The bullet points could then be used as talking points.

3. Title

    The title does not tell the audience the key insight. It makes the presentation sound dry—just information transmission—not something worth remembering.

4. Key message

    What do you think the key message of this slide is? Perhaps it is that sales representative number 4 is extremely effective. How does the slide support this?

5. Chart design

    Refer back to the **design standards** (see Chapter IV) and note where improvements can be made.

 If you are feeling ambitious, you can download the slide from http://becomingvisual.com/portfolio/slideredesign and redesign it. Go to the end of the chapter to see the steps I took to redesign the slide.

Table 7.1 Areas of improvement based on the design standards

Design standard	Needs improvement
Chart format	x
Color	x
Text and labels	x
Readability	x
Scales	x
Data integrity	x
Chartjunk	x
Data density	
Data richness	
Attribution	x

7.1. Using Presentation Software

Individuals and teams in business, academia, and professional settings are tasked with delivering presentations that are both compelling and persuasive. Most of the time, this involves the use of data to provide evidence. In preparation, many of us create PowerPoint slides and write up talking points.

How do you use PowerPoint? Select all that apply.

A. To support your presentation and discussion
B. To serve as your talking points
C. To use as handouts for your audience
D. All of the above

If you selected option A, you are on the right track! If you selected option B and/or C, read the next section, which demonstrates why those options are less than ideal.

PowerPoint slides should not serve as the speaker's notes or the audience's. Figure 7.2 is an all too common example of how slide presentations are designed and delivered. Don't design presentation slides to serve as the speaker's teleprompter.

The presenter should memorize the talking points. This also demonstrates confidence and comfort with the content. When you are reading directly from notes, you lose eye contact with your audience; as a consequence, their attention may drift.

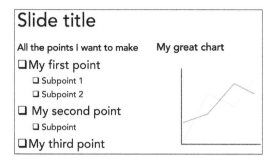

Figure 7.2 An example of a slide used as a teleprompter for the presenter

Using PowerPoint slides as a handout for your audience is a telltale sign that there is way too much information on your slides.

 At the beginning of most presentations, you'll notice a hand in the audience. Usually that person will ask if the slides will be provided. Always prepare to provide slides for your audience at the end of the presentation. You also may want to provide a handout at the beginning of the presentation to circumvent this question. To answer, simply explain that all salient information is provided in the handout and that the slides will be provided after the presentation for reference.

Presentation software should be used to support you as the speaker. It is not meant to provide handouts or be used as a teleprompter. You should speak to your audience to elaborate and explain, rather than write the message on the slides. If you insert everything onto the slides, what's left for you to say? Worse, this impedes the audience's retention of the information you are presenting. Refer back to the discussion on minimizing information overload in Chapter VI.

7.2 Designing Slide Presentations With Visualizations

Whether you use PowerPoint, Keynote, Prezi, or Google Slides, good slide design is essential for organizing and presenting visual content.

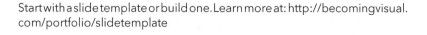 Start with a slide template or build one. Learn more at: http://becomingvisual.com/portfolio/slidetemplate

Alternatives to PowerPoint include Keynote and Google Slides. Keynote offers the ability to create animated charts. Google Slides is a web-based alternative.

Design your slides like a pro by keeping in mind these guiding principles:

DESIGN FOR THE PROJECTOR

PowerPoint should be optimized for the projector being used, rather than for a tablet, paper handouts, or a computer screen.

ASPECT RATIO

Selecting the proper aspect ratio is easy. Use 16:9 for widescreen projectors and 4:3 for standard displays (see Table 7.2).

In PowerPoint, set the aspect ratio by going to FILE > PAGE SETUP and select the appropriate slide size (see Figure 7.3).

Keep the Visual Aesthetics Simple and Readable

Table 7.2 Comparison of the 16:9 to the 4:3 aspect ratio for slide presentations

16:9 aspect ratio

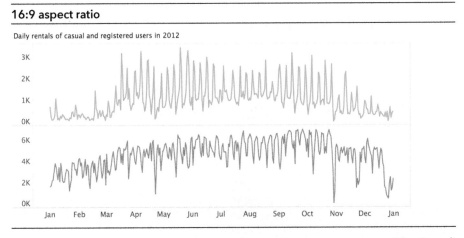

(Continued)

Table 7.2 (Continued)

4:3 aspect ratio

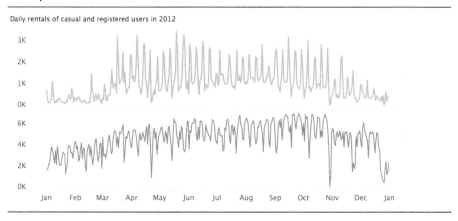

Daily rentals of casual and registered users in 2012

Figure 7.3 A dialogue box in PowerPoint for configuring the aspect ratio

Arial

Helvetica

Avenir Next

Verdana

Figure 7.4 Examples of sans serif fonts

SLIDE BACKGROUND

Use a white background with black text or vice versa. For images, match the slide background to the color of the data graphic as shown in Table 7.3.

Table 7.3 Comparison of a slide with a point map with black text and a white background to a slide with white text and a black background

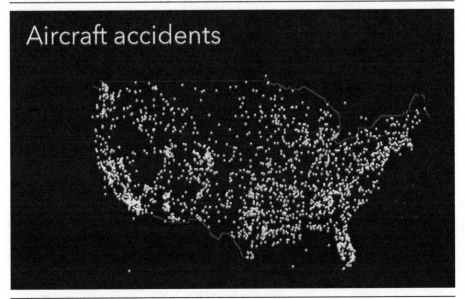

FONT SIZE

Be kind to your audience by making text easy to read. Small text on slides usually only benefits the speaker or those sitting close to the projected slide. Chart labels should be at least 16-point font. Use at least 32-point font for slide titles and 24-point font or larger for bullet points. If 24-point font size seems too large, you are probably including too much text.

FONT FACE

Use a sans serif font such as Arial, Helvetica, Verdana, or Avenir Next (as used throughout this book). Sans serif fonts are considered among the most legible, and Verdana, in particular, is among the most preferred.

COLOR

Color is a powerful way to capture your audience's attention. Just be sure you don't overuse it. Keep slides and charts simple by using a color that contrasts with the slide background or text to highlight an important point. For example, in Table 7.4, a single series is in green to distinguish it from the rest. When the image is converted to grayscale, the highlighted series still stands out from the other lines.

Table 7.4 The use of color to highlight a data series versus a grayscale version of the same chart

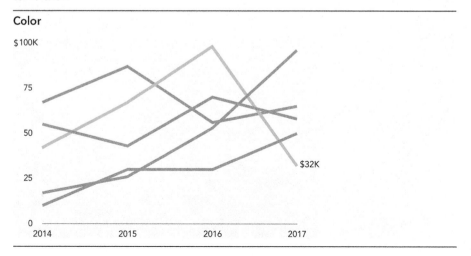

Grayscale

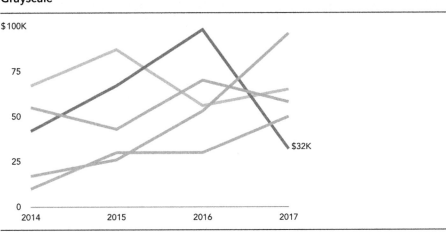

Ensure colors are sufficiently contrasting. You can test this by printing your slides out in black and white. The colors used should be different shades of gray that are distinguishable from one another.

SLIDE AND CHART TITLES

Use sentence-case lettering. Avoid upper- and mixed-case lettering for slide headings. Only capitalize the first letter of the first word for titles, as illustrated below:

Sentence case: Welcome to the course
Title case: Welcome to the Course

Organize and Format the Slides to Maximize Viewing

LAYOUT

Select a slide layout that maximizes the view of your content. Avoid using the standard layout for all content. For example, in Table 7.5, a two-column layout is used for comparisons.

- Use the entire slide for one chart.
- Make the chart as big as possible.
- Keep annotations to a minimum.

Table 7.5 Comparison of different layout styles

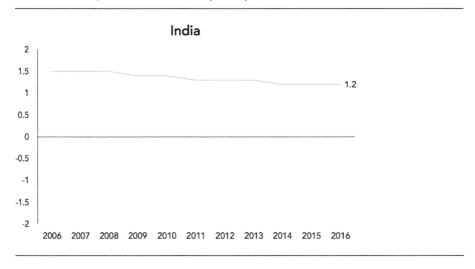

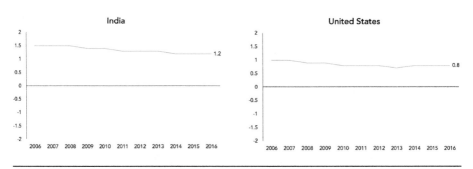

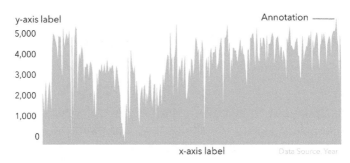

Figure 7.5 A slide with an area chart that fills the entire width of the slide

SLIDE TRANSITIONS

Use simple slide transitions, such as the fade or cut, to move from one slide to the next. Avoid using distracting slide transitions such as the "checkerboard" or "blinds." These transitions do not add to your message; they detract from the message with unnecessary animation and movement.

For example, the slides below compare how the content looks in the middle of a "checkerboard" slide transition versus a fade transition (see Table 7.6).

A Slide Is No Substitute for the Speaker, Nor Should It Be

Presentation software offers many features and options for formatting, designing, and organizing content. Be judicious in selecting which features to add. Some of the special effects add little and may even detract from the message.

TEXT

For text, try to follow the 1-6-6 rule: Only have one idea per slide, keep the slide to six lines, and six words per line (see Figure 7.6)

(John Zimmer, 2010). Ideally, keep text to a minimum. This will help keep the audience's attention on the message of the presentation rather than just the text on the slides.

ANIMATION

Animate content to show the evolution of a trend, pattern, or process. For example, Table 7.7 illustrates the six stages in the beer brewing process. The first stage, milling, is highlighted. At this point in the presentation, the speaker can describe the milling stage, and then use animation to highlight the mashing stage, and so on.

Avoid animating too many objects on the screen simultaneously. This may make it difficult for your audience to follow along.

IMAGES AND ARTWORK

Use images that add to the presentation (including attribution). Avoid using clip art. Consider using creative commons licensed images. For

Table 7.6 The "checkerboard" transition on the left and the "fade" transition on the right

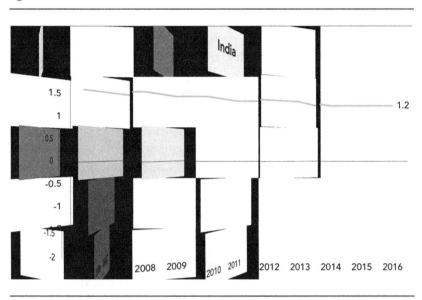

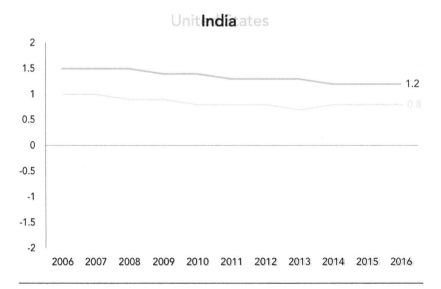

1-6-6 rule

- ❏ This slide follows the rule
- ❏ Only one idea per slide
- ❏ Only six bullet points per slide
- ❏ Only six words per bullet point
- ❏ Use this format sparingly
- ❏ Add visual variety with other elements

Figure 7.6 Guideline for text on slides

Table 7.7 The stages in the beer brewing process, with milling highlighted in the first slide and mashing highlighted in the second slide

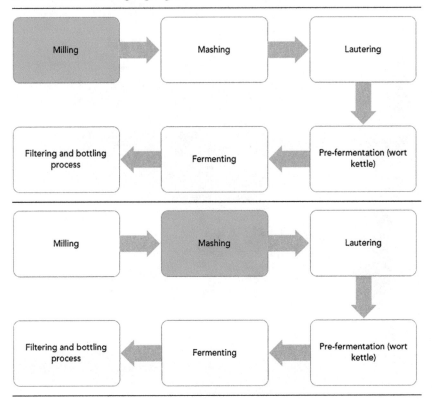

example, if you wanted a map of New York City neighborhoods (see Figure 7.7), search https://search.creativecommons.org

GRAPHICS

Show structures, processes, and flows with graphic charts (e.g., smart art). Avoid adding shadows and minimize the use of color. Refer back to Table 7.7, which shows the six stages of the beer brewing process.

New York City neighborhoods

Source: M. Minderhoud [CC BY-SA 2.5 (http://creativecommons.org/licenses/by-sa/2.5)], Via Wikimedia Commons

Figure 7.7 A creative commons licensed image of New York City

Temperature	Humidity	Wind speed	Casual	Registered	Total rentals
0.637646	0.770417	0.171025	774	4061	4835
0.693829	0.7075	0.172262	661	3846	4507
0.693833	0.703333	0.238804	746	4044	4790
0.656583	0.573333	0.222025	969	4022	4991
0.643313	0.483333	0.209571	1782	3420	5202
0.637629	0.513333	0.0945333	1920	3385	5305

Figure 7.8 Guideline for numbers on slides

TABLES

Use tables to organize information (for example, to show rows and columns of data). For slide presentations, keep the table size to a maximum of six columns by six rows (Paradi, 2017).

VIDEOS

Use brief "explainer" videos to introduce complex processes or concepts. Videos should be under three minutes. If possible, embed the video within the presentation. Playing the video directly in the slide minimizes disruption (instead of opening a new program, like your browser, to link to YouTube, for example).

7.3 Testing Your Presentation

PLAN FOR FAILURE

Bring a backup of your slides on a USB drive and email yourself a copy. Never rely on the technical team to have the right adapter for your laptop. Bring your own HDMI and VGA adapters for your laptop. If you need sound, ensure there are speakers available by requesting them in advance. Bring your own clicker to advance through the slides.

FUNCTIONALITY TEST

Test your slides out beforehand in the actual room in which you will be presenting them. Check to ensure all links, audio, video, and animations are working as they should. Ensure the projector displays your slides with the appropriate screen resolution.

READABILITY TEST

Ensure all slides are readable from the back of the room.

7.4 Delivering Presentations

Putting a good presentation together takes time and effort. It's important to leave time to practice delivering your presentation. Practicing your presentation and honing your message will build your confidence in your idea. Only when you're familiar with the concepts in your presentation, will you be prepared to speak no matter the conditions. On presentation day, follow the tips below to present like a pro.

CLICKER

Use a wireless remote to advance through your slides. This will allow you to move freely around the room as you are presenting, rather than just standing in front of your laptop.

PROJECTION

Always show your slides in full screen using slide show in PowerPoint; this is called Slide Show View. This will maximize the slide for the entire projected area. The audience does not need to see anything but the slide (see Table 7.8).

SPEAKER NOTES

View your slides in presenter view (see Figure 7.9) to see your notes and project the sideshow view to your audience.

SPEAKER POSITION

Avoid standing in front of the slides or behind the podium. Try to move around the room.

PRESENTER NARRATION

Avoid reading off the slides; use your talking points. Talking points should be memorized and included in the notes field in the slide presentation.

Table 7.8 Comparison of the *Normal View* in PowerPoint to the *Slide Show View*

Normal View

Slide Show View

LIVE DEMOS

If you must give a live demonstration of your data graphic as part of your presentation, ensure you have the material cued up and ready before you start. Also, try to present the demo after you complete the presentation.

As an alternative, pre-record "demonstrations" and embed them in the slideshow (at least as a backup). Below are three screenshots of a pre-recorded screencast of an animated data graphic.

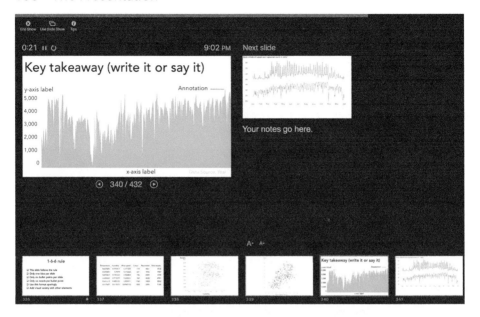

Figure 7.9 Presenter view in PowerPoint

Many interactive or animated visualizations must be shown through a web browser or the native application in which it was created. Stopping a presentation to launch another application is disruptive to the flow of a slide presentation. Instead, pre-record the animation or interaction that you want to show during the live presentation. Embed the recording in your slide presentation.

Learn more at: http://becomingvisual.com/portfolio/screencast

MICROPHONE

Use a microphone. Do not assume that everyone will be able to hear you, even if you think you can speak loud enough.

Not everyone will speak up if they cannot hear you. Using a microphone is even more important if the presentation is being recorded.

HANDOUTS

Avoid printing out each slide in a handout; consider a one-page handout that summarizes your main points instead.

Frame 1

Deadly civil aviation accidents in the United States in 2004

Figure 7.10 An animated data graphic embedded in PowerPoint, shown frame by frame

Frame 2

Deadly civil aviation accidents in the United States in 2005

Figure 7.10 Continued

Frame 3

Deadly civil aviation accidents in the United States in 2006

Figure 7.10 Continued

TAKING QUESTIONS

Decide how you will handle questions. Will you take questions at the end or throughout your presentation?

KEEP TIME

Give yourself a time limit for the presentation that allows time for questions. Bring a watch, your phone, or use the clock in the room to keep track of your time.

7.5 Common Presentation Pitfalls

In my professional lifetime, I have observed many avoidable presentation pitfalls. Here are the 10 most common pitfalls and how you can avoid them.

- Pitfall #1—not sharing your work with others prior to your presentation

  How to avoid it: always ask others for feedback on your slides and charts. This will save you a lot of time in the long run. Ask others for feedback on your presentation style, slide design, and overall content.

- Pitfall #2–lack of audience engagement

  How to avoid it: include opportunities for audience interaction, questions, or conversation.

- Pitfall #3–little or no eye contact with the audience

  How to avoid it: do not look past the audience, or down at your notes. Instead, make eye contact with the audience members.

- Pitfall #4–making your work unreadable (small font)

  How to avoid it: keep bulleted text to 24-point font. Keep chart labels to a minimum of 16-point font.

- Pitfall #5–over the time limit. The speaker did not complete the presentation within the time allotted.

  How to avoid it: rehearse. Record yourself giving the presentation (using screencasting or audio recording software) to measure the length of your presentation. If you run overtime, identify slides to cut and add any additional content (to your notes or slide deck) as needed.

- Pitfall #6–showing too much information on a single slide

  How to avoid it: for text, the guideline is six words per line, and no more than six lines of text per slide (Zimmer, 2010). Tables of numbers should not exceed six columns by six rows (Paradi, 2017). For charts, show full screen and keep annotations to a minimum.

- Pitfall #7–failing to use appropriate data graphics to show insights

  How to avoid it: show clear data trends, patterns, and insights with charts. Use encodings and preattentive attributes to highlight the area of interest.

- Pitfall #8–showing a chart without an explanation

  How to avoid it: explain any chart that is included in the presentation; otherwise, do not include it.

- Pitfall #9–presenting a chart without a clear takeaway

  How to avoid it: only use charts that clearly show a trend, relationship, comparison, or composition. Force yourself to write the key takeaway in the slide title or the slide notes.

- Pitfall #10–showing so many variables on a single visual display that they impair the readability of the chart or graph

  How to avoid it: use animation or slide transitions to show the variables of interest at the point they are relevant to the presentation.

7.6 After Your Presentation

Determine if and how you will share your slides with the audience.

If you want to share your slides with others after the presentation, there are many platforms available for uploading and sharing slide presentations. Learn more at: http://becomingvisual.com/portfolio/slidesharing/

You can prepare stellar presentations by avoiding the pitfalls discussed in this chapter and using the guidelines to inform your design. With any presentation, whether you are delivering it or are in a position to critique it, consider these questions:

☐ Did the speaker select an interesting story to tell with the data as it related to her topic and audience?
☐ Did the speaker select visualizations (chart types) to present her data?
☐ Did the speaker apply effective design principles to her charts to clearly present her data?
☐ Did the speaker apply effective design principles to her charts and the presentation?
☐ Did the speaker use visualizations that worked together to tell a coherent story?

7.7 Presentation Checklist

DESIGNING YOUR SLIDE PRESENTATION

☐ Design for the projector: PowerPoint should be optimized for the projector being used, rather than for a tablet, paper handouts, or a computer screen.
☐ Aspect ratio: use 16:9 for widescreen and 4:3 for standard displays.

☐ Slide background color: use a white background with black text or vice versa.

☐ Font size: use at least 32-point font for slide titles and 24-point font or larger for bullet points.

☐ Font face: use a sans serif font such as Arial, Helvetica, Verdana, or Avenir Next

☐ Color: keep slides and charts simple by using a color that contrasts with the slide background or text to highlight an important point.

☐ Slide and chart titles: use sentence case lettering. Avoid upper and mixed-case lettering for slide headings.

☐ Layout: select a slide layout that maximizes the view of your content.

☐ Slide transitions: use simple slide transitions, such as the fade or cut, to move from one slide to the next. Avoid using distracting slide transitions such as the "checkerboard" or "blinds."

☐ Text: Follow the 1-6-6 rule—only have one idea per slide, keep the slide to six lines, and six words per line.

☐ Animation: animate content to show the evolution of a trend, pattern, or process.

☐ Images and artwork: use images that add to the presentation (and with attribution). Avoid using clip art.

☐ Graphics: show structures, processes, and flows with graphic charts (e.g., smart art).

☐ Tables: use tables to organize information. Keep the table size to a maximum of six columns by six rows.

☐ Videos: use brief "explainer" videos to introduce complex processes or concepts.

TESTING YOUR PRESENTATION

☐ Plan for failure: bring a backup of your slides on a USB drive and email yourself a copy.

☐ Functionality test: test your slides out beforehand in the actual room in which you will be presenting them.

☐ Readability test: ensure all slides are readable from the back of the room.

DELIVERING YOUR PRESENTATION

☐ Clicker: use a wireless remote to advance through your slides.

☐ Projection: always show your slides in full screen using slide show in PowerPoint; this is called Slide Show View.

☐ Speaker notes: view your slides in presenter view to see your notes and project the sideshow view to your audience.

☐ Speaker position: avoid standing in front of the slides or behind the podium. Try to move around the room.

☐ Presenter narration: avoid reading off the slides; use your talking points. Talking points should be memorized and included in the notes field in the slide presentation.

☐ Live demos: if you must give a live demonstration of your data graphic as part of your presentation, ensure you have the material cued up and ready before you start.

☐ Microphone: use a microphone. Do not assume that everyone will be able to hear you, even if you think you can speak loud enough.

☐ Handouts: avoid printing out each slide in a handout; consider a one-page handout that summarizes your main points instead.

☐ Questions: decide how you will handle questions. Will you take questions at the end or throughout your presentation?

☐ Keep time: give yourself a time limit for the presentation that allows time for questions.

AFTER YOUR PRESENTATION

• Sharing your slides: determine if and how you will share your slides with the audience.

7.8 Exercise

1. Review Figure 7.1. Redesign the slide to show the stellar performance of sales representative 4. Download the data from http://becomingvisual.com/portfolio/slideredesign

   Here is my redesign:

Table 7.9 A revision of the slide shown in Figure 7.1

Original slide with bulleted list items removed and chart enlarged	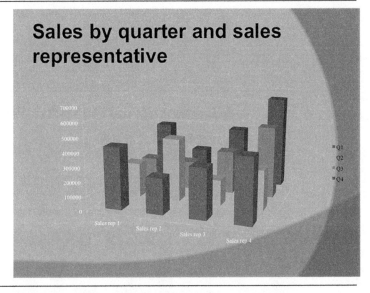
Step 1: Removed background graphic; changed it to white; removed text to show full slide	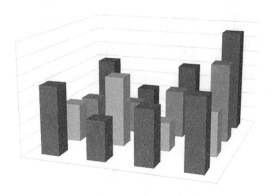

Table 7.9 (Continued)

Step 2: Removed 3D bars and used a 2D graph	**Sales by quarter and sales representative** 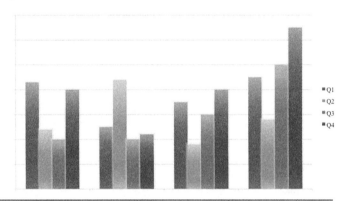
Step 3: Changed the font color for all labels to black to increase visibility and readability	**Sales by quarter and sales representative** 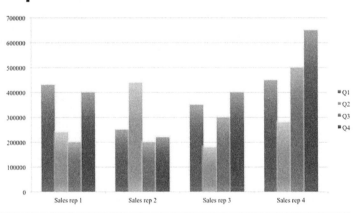

Step 4: Added
commas to the
y-axis values

Sales by quarter and sales representative

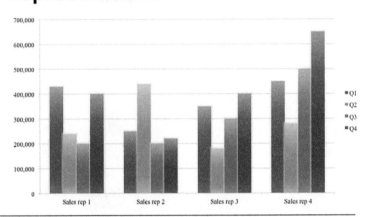

Sales by quarter and sales representative

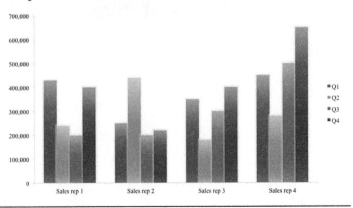

Table 7.9 (Continued)

Step 6: Re-shaded column bars from lightest to darkest	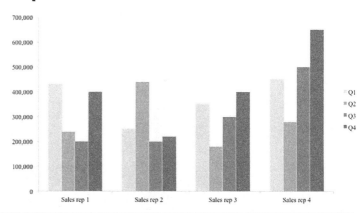
Step 7: Changed label font from a serif to a sans serif font	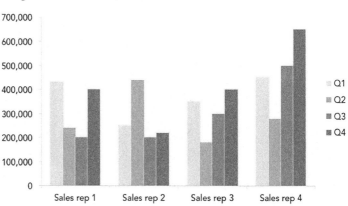

Table 7.9 (Continued)

Step 8: Removed tick marks and unnecessary axis lines

Sales by quarter and sales representative

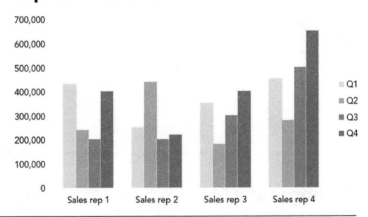

Step 9: Changed the chart type to a horizontal bar to show rank order

Sales by quarter and sales representative

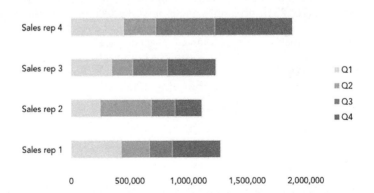

Table 7.9 (Continued)

| Step 10: Moved legend to top of chart; labeled Q4 values as a reference point; re-ordered sale representatives to show highest to lowest from top to bottom; used the sales representative's name rather than Sales Rep 1, Rep 2, . . . Rep 4 | 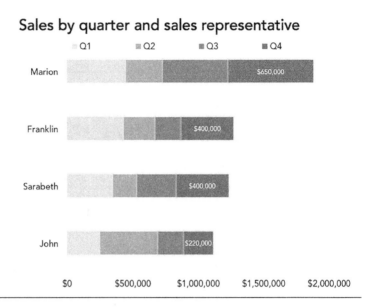 |

Bibliography

Akinson, C., & Mayer, R. (2004). Five ways to reduce PowerPoint overload. Retrieved from http://www.bhertz.nl/wp-content/uploads/2011/07/atkinson_mayer_power-point_4_23_04.pdf

Bernard, M., Lida, B., Riley, S., Hackler, T., & Janzen, K. (2002). A comparison of popular online fonts: Which size and type is best? Retrieved from http://usabilitynews.org/a-comparison-of-popular-online-fonts-which-size-and-type-is-best

Paradi, D. (2017). Using graphs and tables on presentation slides. Retrieved from www.thinkoutsidetheslide.com/using-graphs-and-tables-on-presentation-slides

Publication manual of the American Psychological Association. (2010). (6th ed., repr. ed.). Washington, DC: American Psychological Association.

Zimmer, J. (2010). PowerPoint math: The 1-6-6 rule. Retrieved from https://mannerof-speaking.org/2010/03/04/powerpoint-math-the-1-6-6-rule

VIII

THE
CASES

How do professionals use data graphics in their work?

Chapter 8 showcases how data and graphics come together to present findings and provide visual evidence. Five distinct case studies highlight a range of approaches to the use of data graphics. The visualizations presented were used by the case authors in their work.

Investigating the predictive power of Twitter data in a presidential election
Andrew Hamlet

Analyzing and presenting predictors of startup success
Prasant Sudhakaran

Reporting on project status
Adam Gonthier

Identifying gaming behavior through analytics
Harry Chernoff

Exploring the opening and closings of NYC schools
Reshama Shaikh and Riyaz Shaikh

Can Twitter predict the outcome of the U.S. presidential election?

Andrew Hamlet

This case uses data graphics to illustrate the analysis of Twitter data to visualize Twitter activity by presidential candidates and their followers.

Introduction

In November 2015, a group of NYU Stern MBA students (Troy Manos, Keita Shimizu, Tarang Dawer, and Andrew Hamlet) set out to study whether Twitter can predict the outcome of a U.S. presidential election. Based on preliminary research into the opinions of major news outlets, the answer was not clear. There are many different viewpoints as to the value of social media, specifically Twitter, in predicting election outcomes. Some news sources saw any publicity as good publicity.

What people say on Twitter or Facebook is a very good indicator of how they will vote.[1]
> –THE WASHINGTON POST

In the 2010 data, our Twitter data predicted the winner in 404 out of 435 competitive [congressional] races.
> –THE WASHINGTON POST

If people must talk about you, even in negative ways, it is a signal that a candidate is on the verge of victory.
> –THE WASHINGTON POST

Others questioned if social media could provide a direct measurement of voter intention. To what extent could interactions on Twitter signal a specific outcome? News sources commented:

Twitter is a notably non-representative sample of people.[2]
> –THE ATLANTIC

At last count, eight percent of American adults use Twitter daily; only 15 percent are on it at all.

—THE ATLANTIC

In the best of circumstances, it is possible to detect the online projections and manifestations of existing offline phenomena that tend to coincide with particular outcomes or events.

—THE ATLANTIC

What Do You Think? How Would You Begin to Explore These Questions?

What data would you need to begin your study?

You could begin with a social graph of each presidential candidate and their followers on Twitter, as in Table 8.1.

This is what the team did. However, the data itself did not present any interesting findings. To better understand the data, we developed a methodology for analyzing the Twitter data. We created three key metrics: 1) volume, 2) engagement, and 3) followers (see Figure 8.1).

Volume was measured using two inputs: 1) the **number of tweets**, defined as the daily count of tweets from the respective profile; and 2) by the **number of mentions,** defined as the daily count of tweets referencing the respective profile.

Engagement was measured by two inputs: 1) the **average retweet per tweet**, defined as the daily average retweets per tweet from the

Table 8.1 A sample of Twitter data collected on the presidential candidates and the volume of tweets, the audience engagement, and Twitter followers

Date	Favorites	Followers	Mentions	Party	Politician	Retweets
2/25/16	2353	6435	5899	Democrat	Bernie Sanders	1106
2/26/16	4455	7209	5016	Democrat	Bernie Sanders	2243
2/27/16	3469	5147	7551	Democrat	Bernie Sanders	1520
2/28/16	0	6144	2901	Democrat	Bernie Sanders	0
6/16/15	1711	7262	7681	Democrat	Hillary Clinton	813
6/17/15	586	6789	6329	Democrat	Hillary Clinton	312
6/18/15	2618	6646	5380	Democrat	Hillary Clinton	1688
6/19/15	1337	6882	4734	Democrat	Hillary Clinton	674
6/20/15	1259	5787	5333	Democrat	Hillary Clinton	959
6/21/15	1915	6464	3950	Democrat	Hillary Clinton	655

Figure 8.1 Methodology for analyzing Twitter data, outlining the three key metrics

respective candidate profile; and 2) the **average favorite per tweet**, which was the daily average favorites per tweet from the respective candidate profile.

Followers were measured by the **number of followers**, defined as the daily number of followers gained by the respective candidate profile.

These metrics were gathered daily from 11/1/2015 to 11/30/2015. Each metric was averaged by month, normalized across the candidates, equally weighted, summed for a **Total Composite Score**, and sorted in descending order to produce a ranking.

1. Averaged by month

    [22, 20, 25, 15, 15, 37, 25, 38, 10, 23, 16, 20, 13, 22, 25, 12, 13, 7, 31, 28, 45, 19, 18, 17, 20, 9, 8, 18, 17, 13]/[30]

    [20]

2. Normalized across candidates, divided by the maximum for each metric

    [20, 10, 10, 12]/[20]

    [1.00, 0.50, 0.50, 0.60]

3. Equally weighted number of tweets + number of mentions + avg. retweet per tweet + avg. favorite per tweet + number of followers

4. Summed for Total Composite Score

    1.00 + 0.93 + 1.00 + 1.00 + 1.00 = 4.93

5. Sorted in descending order to produce a ranking

The team appended the original data table to its new metrics, TW Followers, TW Mentions, TW Retweets, TW Tweets, and Composite Score (see Table 8.2).

Using this methodology, the team conducted an analysis of leading candidates from both political parties for the 2016 Presidential Election. We showed what the presidential race looked like on Twitter based on team analysis (see Figure 8.2). The heat map suggests

Table 8.2 Calculated fields used as inputs into the Total Composite Score

Date	Politician	TW Favorites	TW Followers	TW Mentions	TW Retweets	TW Tweets	Composite Score
2/25/16	Bernie Sanders	0.165996473	0.168178136	0.092417359	0.106571594	0.169230769	0.70239433
2/26/16	Bernie Sanders	0.314285714	0.188406555	0.078583738	0.216130276	0.107692308	0.90509859
2/27/16	Bernie Sanders	0.244726631	0.134516374	0.118298606	0.146463673	0.076923077	0.720928361
2/28/16	Bernie Sanders	0	0.160572877	0.045448849	0	0	0.206021726
6/16/15	Hillary Clinton	0.120705467	0.189791705	0.120335266	0.078338794	0.107692308	0.616863539
6/17/15	Hillary Clinton	0.041340388	0.177429893	0.099154003	0.030063596	0.169230769	0.517218649
6/18/15	Hillary Clinton	0.184691358	0.173692601	0.084286386	0.162651763	0.076923077	0.682245185
6/19/15	Hillary Clinton	0.094320988	0.17986044	0.074165753	0.064945076	0.169230769	0.582523025
6/20/15	Hillary Clinton	0.088818342	0.151242715	0.083550055	0.092407015	0.092307692	0.508325819
6/21/15	Hillary Clinton	0.135097002	0.168936048	0.061883127	0.06311428	0.092307692	0.521338149

	Followers	Retweets	Favorites	Mentions	Tweets	Total	Rank	
Donald Trump	1.00	0.93	1.00	1.00	1.00	4.93	1	Normalized ranges for each metric
Hillary Clinton	0.95	0.54	0.43	0.50	0.52	2.94	2	■ .75 to 1
Bernie Sanders	0.20	1.00	0.80	0.05	0.53	2.58	3	■ .50 to .74
Ted Cruz	0.12	0.32	0.19	0.51	0.59	1.74	4	■ .25 to .49
Ben Carson	0.21	0.31	0.31	0.30	0.23	1.37	5	□ 0 to .24
Marco Rubio	0.20	0.22	0.19	0.29	0.19	1.09	6	
Jeb Bush	0.08	0.06	0.05	0.17	0.48	0.84	7	
Carly Fiorina	0.13	0.09	0.08	0.17	0.14	0.61	8	
Martin O'Malley	0.02	0.05	0.04	0.06	0.33	0.50	9	

Figure 8.2 A heat map displaying Twitter activity across the presidential candidates, with Donald Trump leading during the time frame 11/1/2015-11/30/2015

Donald Trump, when compared to the other candidates, maximized his Twitter presence. Additionally, the heat map shows that the primary presidential race (as viewed on Twitter) was closer between Democrats than it was among Republicans.

The heat map presents the rank of each candidate according to the calculated metrics. The darker shading was used to indicate relative leadership in a category when compared to others. The metrics are divided into four subgroups that correspond to the ranges 1 to .75, .74 to 50, .49 to .25, and .24 to 0. Each subgroup was assigned a shade of green.

After analyzing the data from November 2015, Andrew determined how the model could adjust over time. He categorized the candidates by political party and applied the methodology to the presidential primaries. Andrew illustrated how the two leading candidates from each party ranked according to the model (from June 2015 through February 2016) (see Figure 8.3).

As of February 2016, Donald Trump was leading Ted Cruz by 1.23, and Hillary Clinton was leading Bernie Sanders by 0.31, both in terms of Total Composite Score. Thus, the line chart presents a smaller gap between Hillary Clinton and Bernie Sanders than between Donald Trump and Ted Cruz.

Around March 2016, as it became clear the president's race would be between Donald Trump and Hillary Clinton, the methodology was applied to the two presidential nominees. The following time series display (see Figure 8.4) illustrates how Donald Trump and Hillary Clinton ranked according to the model, by month, from June 2015 through October 2016.

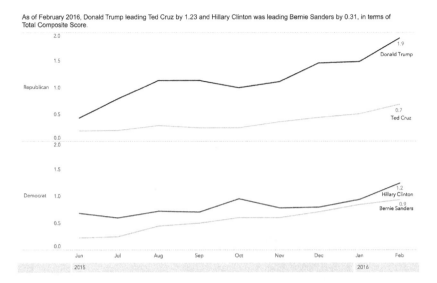

As of February 2016, Donald Trump leading Ted Cruz by 1.23 and Hillary Clinton was leading Bernie Sanders by 0.31, in terms of Total Composite Score.

Figure 8.3 Time series of social media behaviors on Twitter showing Donald Trump leading Ted Cruz, and Hillary Clinton more narrowly leading Bernie Sanders, through February 2016

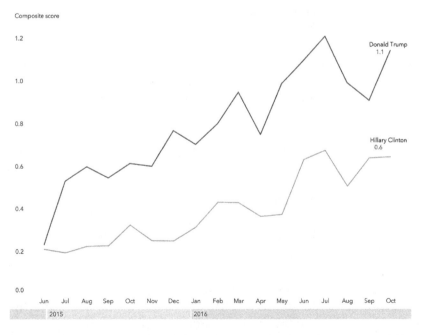

Figure 8.4 Time series of social media behaviors on Twitter showing Donald Trump leading Hillary Clinton throughout the primary and general campaigns

Donald Trump went on to win the 2016 presidential election. Many cite social media as a contributing factor in the outcome. Or perhaps the insights presented are more indicative of Clinton's defeat than Trump's win?

August 6, 2017

Everyone understands that what gets shared online matters now.[3]

　　　　　　　　　　　　　　　　　–THE NEW YORK TIMES

July 8, 2017

Given the role that Twitter played in the presidential campaign, we analyzed Mr. Trump's and Mrs. Clinton's Twitter accounts in the six months before the election. We found that Mr. Trump benefited by using moral-emotional language (a 15 percent increase in retweets) but Mrs. Clinton did not.[4]

　　　　　　　　　　　　　　　　　–THE NEW YORK TIMES

During the election, the prevailing belief was Trump would not win. However, this study used a model based on Twitter data of the presidential candidates and found that it mirrored the election outcome. This analysis also raised more questions, such as:

- Who engaged on Twitter with Donald Trump?
- Is there something about the content of the tweets that led the audience to engage?
- If Twitter represents mass public opinion, why did the engagement rates not translate into the popular vote?
- What is the relationship between social and traditional media?

The case presented uses data visualization to present the results of a research project. The visualizations were created in Tableau. This case was also presented at The New York Chapter of the American Association for Public Opinion Research in early 2016.

Can you predict the success of a startup?

Prasant Sudhakaran

In this case, you'll see how data graphics are used by Aingel Corp. to showcase key predictors of successful teams to potential investors.

Why does one startup venture receive early stage funding rather than another? Is it possible to predict which venture will outperform others? The National Venture Capital Association reported that 1,444 out of 679,072[5] companies in the United States had secured initial capital in 2015. This is less than 0.5%of all startups. How does an investor differentiate between a Blockchain-based money transfer app based in New York, for example, and an app with similar features based in Palo Alto?

At Aingel Corp.,[6] we observed that investing in a startup is more often based on an investor's "hunch" or "gut feeling" than on data such as an industry-wide metric. Our clients are early stage venture capital funds (VCs) such as Endure Capital.[7] VCs typically have two competing considerations when deciding whether to fund a new idea:

1. Low probability of a hit: they have to invest in a wide array of projects for a reasonable return on their investment, and still be extremely selective, to ensure their portfolio is of a high quality.
2. Fear of missing out: due to their selectivity, they might miss out on "home runs" like Facebook, Uber, Pinterest, etc.

To mitigate the risk of missing out or not diversifying their investments, VCs use crude markers to filter out firms. Such metrics include:

*   alumni of top schools
*   startup experience
*   fundraising experience

Inherent biases may influence decision making. For example, looking for a particular archetype of a founder (e.g., the next Zuckerberg/Musk) could overshadow other successful archetypes that investors have not yet encountered.

While startups with analytics-based solutions are at the height of popularity, analytics have not significantly influenced the venture capital (VC) industry. Aingel saw this an opportunity to use data analytics to **predict start up success**.

Our working hypothesis was that teams are the most important part of a startup. Endure Capital knew the importance of the team. Many investors believe that it is better to invest in a stellar team with a mediocre idea than in a stellar idea driven by a middling team.[8]

We tested our hypothesis using data acquired through our data partner (Crunchbase), as well as via publicly available tweets on Twitter belonging to 5,348 founders across 4,061 startups founded between 2003 and 2013.

The Insight and Proof of Concept

First, we needed to determine if there was a relationship between an entrepreneur's personality and the amount of funding raised. Essentially, we had to show statistical significance. We did this by studying the amount of funding raised, and a variety of personality attributes.

The findings revealed that there were clear differences in personality traits among founders relative to the amount of funding they raise. Large differences were noted for companies with cumulative funding of $5 million, $50 million, and $100 million. Furthermore, the greater the funding, the wider the range of personality attributes that are significant in founder groups. This means that despite superficial similarities, such as school attended, or occupational history, different levels of success had very different personality traits related to them.

We knew we had to crystallize these findings for VC clients. We wanted to persuade them to use our services to help inform their investments. We sought to show evidence that there is a relationship between the amount of funding a startup receives and the personality traits of its founder(s).

Figure 8.5 shows screens from an interactive dashboard created in Tableau.

Each screen shows multiple boxplots, each representing a different personality including agreeableness, conscientiousness, emotional range, extraversion, and openness. The median score for each trait of founders who raised money over the threshold is shown with a green bubble. This allowed for easy comparison of the founders' traits to the

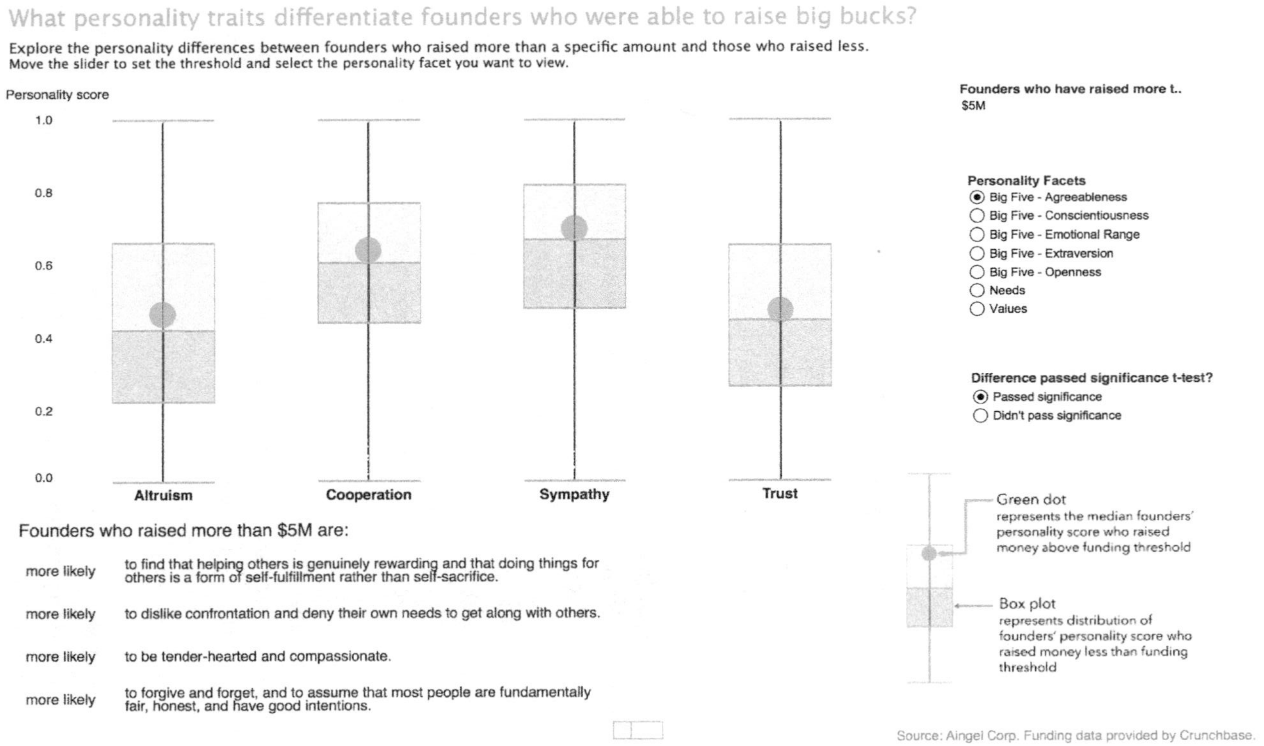

Figure 8.5 An interactive Tableau dashboard used to show the relationship between funding and personality traits of startup founders

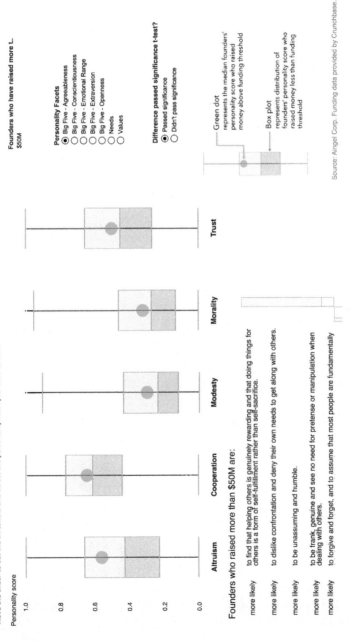

Figure 8.5 Continued

What personality traits differentiate founders who were able to raise big bucks?

Explore the personality differences between founders who raised more than a specific amount and those who raised less.
Move the slider to set the threshold and select the personality facet you want to view.

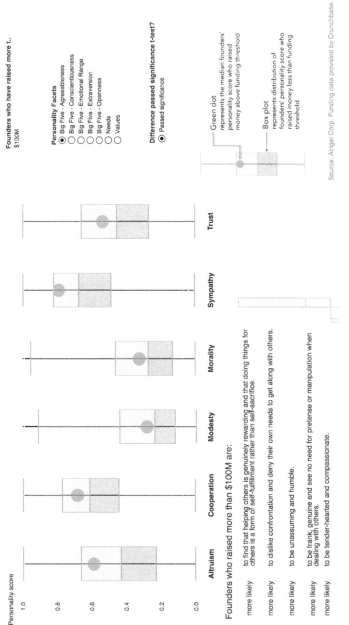

Founders who have raised more t..
$100M

Personality Facets
- Big Five - Agreeableness
- Big Five - Conscientiousness
- Big Five - Emotional Range
- Big Five - Extraversion
- Big Five - Openness
- Needs
- Values

Difference passed significance t-test?
- Passed significance

Green dot
represents the median founders'
personality score who raised
money above funding threshold

Box plot
represents distribution of
founders' personality score who
raised money less than funding
threshold

Source: Aingel Corp. Funding data provided by Crunchbase.

Personality score

1.0
0.8
0.6
0.4
0.2
0.0

Altruism   Cooperation   Modesty   Morality   Sympathy   Trust

Founders who raised more than $100M are:

more likely   to find that helping others is genuinely rewarding and that doing things for others is a form of self-fulfillment rather than self-sacrifice.

more likely   to dislike confrontation and deny their own needs to get along with others.

more likely   to be unassuming and humble.

more likely   to be frank, genuine and see no need for pretense or manipulation when dealing with others.

more likely   to be tender-hearted and compassionate.

Figure 8.5 Continued

What personality traits differentiate founders who were able to raise big bucks?

Explore the personality differences between founders who raised more than a specific amount and those who raised less. Move the slider to set the threshold and select the personality facet you want to view.

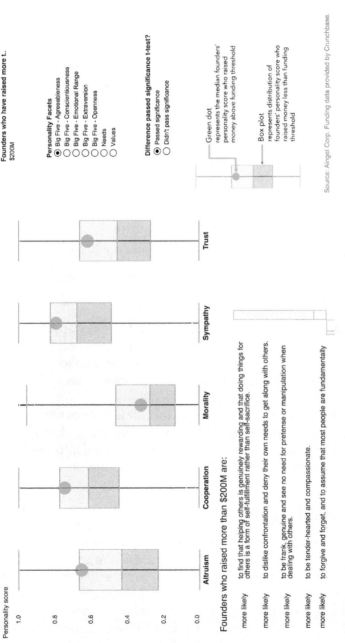

Founders who have raised more t...
$200M

Personality Facets
- ◉ Big Five - Agreeableness
- ◯ Big Five - Conscientiousness
- ◯ Big Five - Emotional Range
- ◯ Big Five - Extraversion
- ◯ Big Five - Openness
- ◯ Needs
- ◯ Values

Difference passed significance t-test?
- ◉ Passed significance
- ◯ Didn't pass significance

Green dot
represents the median founders' personality score who raised money above funding threshold

Box plot
represents distribution of founders' personality score who raised money less than funding threshold

Source: Aingel Corp. Funding data provided by Crunchbase.

Personality score

Altruism   Cooperation   Morality   Sympathy   Trust

Founders who raised more than $200M are:

more likely   to find that helping others is genuinely rewarding and that doing things for others is a form of self-fulfillment rather than self-sacrifice.

more likely   to dislike confrontation and deny their own needs to get along with others.

more likely   to be frank, genuine and see no need for pretense or manipulation when dealing with others.

more likely   to be tender-hearted and compassionate.

more likely   to forgive and forget, and to assume that most people are fundamentally

Figure 8.5 Continued

Founders who have raised more than

$200M

○ < >

Personality Facets

○ Big Five - Agreeableness
◉ Big Five - Conscientiousness
○ Big Five - Emotional Range
○ Big Five - Extraversion
○ Big Five - Openness
○ Needs
○ Values

Figure 8.6 Interactive features in Tableau for filtering

distribution of other founders that have raised more than the target amount of funding needed.

The agreeableness of founders who have raised $5m
The agreeableness of founders who have raised $50m
The agreeableness of founders who have raised $100m
The agreeableness of founders who have raised $200m

The interactive features included sliders and radio buttons to filter personality traits related to the amount of funding raised (see Figure 8.6). The threshold or range was divided into the following bins: 0–5M, 50M–99M, 100M–199M, 200M and beyond.

The Challenge

Building on this proof of concept, Aingel worked to create the industry metric for predicting startup success. We reviewed the profiles of startup ventures across educational, work, and entrepreneurial history. In addition, we built an algorithm that deduces personality archetype scores to predict the success of a team at inception. An "Inception Score" is calculated using a patent pending algorithm–a score for the startup members (individually), and combined (as a team), to predict their success. It uses a scale of 0 to 100, the higher the score, the greater the probability of success.

Building an Interface for Clients

Aingel needed to provide a way for its clients to use the inception score and the personality traits to inform their investment decisions. The prototype illustrated by Figure 8.5 was complex and not intended to be used by Aingel's clients. How could Aingel provide an interface that would enable its clients to evaluate specific startups in terms of the founder's personality traits?

How Could You Help Aingel Design This Interface? What Types of Data Graphics Would Be Useful to Its Clients?

WHAT DID WE DO?

We created an online platform that visualized the scores individually for each entrepreneur. This was done via Radar Plots in D3, with the charts created dynamically using React. Table 8.3 shows the inception scores of well-known startups The Muse, Uber, and Airbnb. The radar charts show the variability of personality traits among founders.

Each radar chart shows the personality traits using a polar coordinate system. Each trait is marked around the circle. Each filled polygon represents a different founder and the degree to which s/he rates high (closer to the edge) or low (closer to the center) for a specific trait. When more than one polygon is presented, it is easy to compare the traits of the founders.

Figures 8.7 and 8.8 show the inception score and founders' personality traits of MedNet, a company that Endure funded. How would you interpret these charts? Note the difference between Nadine and Samir. Nadine rates high on trust, while Samir rates high on imagination, but lower on trust.

While the charts presented a small subset of available personality traits, Endure's general partner Tarek Fahim commented that these descriptions "largely made sense." He also added that it was humanly impossible to discern these factors without access to the inception score and the visualizations of founders' personalities. Investment professionals need data-driven tools at their service.

Later in 2017, Tarek and his team evaluated potential investments using Aingel's platform, and ended up investing in four startups from the January 2017 cohort at the startup incubator Y Combinator.

Tarek noted, "Y Combinator is very competitive and needs to make fast decisions to get to the best companies before others. Aingel

Table 8.3 The inception scores of The Muse, Uber, and Airbnb with one of the founder's personality traits highlighted

The Muse

The Muse ▣ 95% Inception Score™ ⓘ

The Muse is the most trusted destination for your career, helping over 50 million people every year find jobs & succeed in their careers.

Alex Cavoulacos's Personality

 Alyssa McCreery
Founder Score: 94%

 Kathryn Minshew
Founder Score: 83%

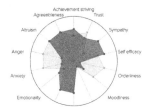 Alex Cavoulacos
Founder Score: 95%

Uber

Uber ▣ 95% Inception Score™ ⓘ

Uber is a mobile app connecting passengers with drivers for hire.

Oscar Salazar's Personality

 Garrett Camp
Founder Score: 94%

 Oscar Salazar
Founder Score: 84%

Travis Kalanick
Founder Score: 85%

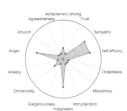

Airbnb

Airbnb ▣ 97% Inception Score™ ⓘ

Airbnb is an online community marketplace for people to list, discover, and book accommodations around the world.

Joe Gebbia's Personality

 Nathan Blecharczyk
Founder Score: 97%

 Joe Gebbia
Founder Score: 63%

 Brian Chesky
Founder Score: 83%

Mednet ■ 80% Inception Score™ ⊙

The Mednet is a network of oncologists who are trying to treat cancer.

Nadine Housri's Personality

Samir Housri
Founder Score: 79%

Nadine Housri
Founder Score: 76%

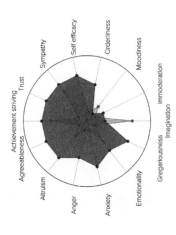

Trust
HIGH: More likely to trust people easily and take them at face value.
LOW: Less likely to trust people easily and take them at face value.

Figure 8.7 Personality traits for one of the founders, Nadine Housri of Mednet

Mednet ▪ 80% Inception Score™ ☺

The Mednet is a network of oncologists who are trying to treat cancer.

Samir Housri's Personality

Samir Housri
Founder Score: 79%

Nadine Housri
Founder Score: 76%

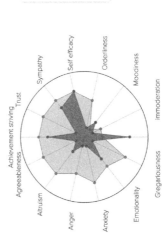

Imagination

HIGH: More likely to view the real world as too ordinary and use their imagination and creativity as a way of creating a richer and more interesting inner-world.

LOW: More likely to prefer facts. Less likely to use their imagination and creativity.

Figure 8.8 Personality traits for one of the founders, Samir Housri of Mednet

helped us in filtering the companies and focusing only on the intersection of 19 companies we originally liked and the 15 companies that
scored higher than approximately 80. The result was only nine companies, which allowed us to focus more easily on our selections.

It also helped us to discover a company we considered a diamond
in the rough. It was not originally one of our selections, but Aingel's
algorithm considered it a worthy investment; we decided to talk to
them and ended up investing."

With changes in government policy, geopolitical shifts, and a mix-
ture of hope and fear in the investment climate, firms like Endure need
every trick in the book to outwit the competition.

Summary

The case presented is an example of using data visualization to showcase evidence to support a hypothesis and implement a web-based
interface to showcase the similarities and differences among company
founders. The data graphics were created in Tableau and D3. The display types include dashboards, interactive charts, and statistical and
multivariate visualizations. The data graphics have been modified by
the author from their original format for purposes of this publication
and printing requirements.

Reporting on project status

Adam Gonthier

Using data visualizations in business reports is commonplace. However, using them to present insights that management can analyze and act upon requires proper data formatting, analysis, and a clear presentation. The objective is to present the information in a quick and easy to understand format. This example shows how data graphics can supply a quick and clear understanding of the status of the project.

Introduction: Project Reporting for a Large-Scale Construction Project[9]

Franklin Yang, a construction manager for a transportation authority organization in the United States, sat in his office late at night pondering a dilemma. He was responsible for managing the commissioning of a large transportation terminal construction project and it was behind schedule. Commissioning is the final phase of a construction project.

This phase is critical because it is where the different systems of the structure, such as heating, cooling, and electrical are brought online into their operational state, and integrated to function together. The project had been under construction for 32 months, and there were only four months remaining until opening day.

A rigorous testing process was put in place to ensure each system met the required design specifications and could be integrated with the other systems. The testing process was comprised of three phases:

1. Pre-Functional Testing: confirm everything has been installed correctly
2. Functional Performance Testing: certify that all systems are active and operating as intended
3. Integrated Systems Testing: ensure the systems are communicating correctly with each other

Table 8.4 Contractors on this project and their areas of expertise

Contractor	Area of Expertise (Trade)	Systems Covered
Warden HVAC	Mechanical	Heating, Cooling & Fire Safety
Penta Power	Electrical	Electrical Power & Wiring
Pontview Telecom	Communications	Internet & Phones
Riptide Controls	Conveyance	Elevators & Parts Retrieval
Tectric Façades	Envelope	Windows, Walls & Roof
Elliot Systems	Industrial	Vehicle Fueling & Washing

Each testing phase required Franklin to track the open issues and their resolution. Any open issue would prevent phase completion.

There were six different contractors involved in the project. Each provided its own expertise in a specialized segment of construction (e.g., mechanical, electrical, and communications) (see Table 8.4). Each contractor was in a different phase of the testing process.

As the point person coordinating all the commissioning activities, Franklin had to relay the project's status to his superiors. His superiors could then make adjustments to get the project back on schedule. Tables 8.5 and 8.6 provide a sample of the data that Franklin collected to use in his report.

Challenge

Franklin needed to report on the status of the commissioning to his managers. His goal was to provide an update on the project's progress that would persuade management to adjust its manpower allocations to meet the project deadline.

How should Franklin prepare his report on commissioning so his superiors can quickly see the project's progress? What visualizations could Franklin use to bring clarity to the situation?

See How Franklin Used Data Visualization as Evidence to Persuade Management to Allocate More Project Resources

Table 8.5 Issue log

System	Deficiency location	Testing phase	Deficiency description	Status
AC Unit	1st Floor Mezz	Pre-Functional	BMS wiring is incomplete. Trane technician is scheduled to complete wiring	Closed
Comm Room Grounding	All Comm Rooms	Functional performance	Jumpers are only secured with one lug; two is required	Open
Comm Room Grounding	All Comm Rooms	Functional performance	Ladder racks are not grounded to the MGB	Open
Comm Room Grounding	All Comm Rooms	Functional performance	A/C Ducts are not grounded	Open
Comm Room Grounding	Comm Room 132	Functional performance	Bonding jumpers are one-lug type; two-hole type jumpers are required	Open
AC Unit	1st Floor Mezz	Pre-Functional	Cover missing on electrical junction box	Closed
AC Unit	1st Floor Mezz	Pre-Functional	Air filters are not installed	Closed
Water Meters	Water Meter Room	Integrated systems	Water meter 1 has greater than 15% error in water volume recorded after a two-hour period. The error must be less than 5%	Open
Security System	Comm Closet 132	Pre-Functional	The UPS wiring is not landed.	Closed

Table 8.6 Open and closed issues

	2013			2014								
	Oct	Nov	Dec	Jan	Feb	Mar	Apr	May	Jun	Jul	Aug	Sept
Open	21	43	211	320	449	477	1,146	1,343	1,734	1,778	1,669	1,575
Closed	0	0	59	76	118	201	202	237	540	771	1,415	1,642
Total	21	43	270	396	567	678	1,348	1,580	2,274	2,549	3,084	3,217

How Did Franklin Use Data Visualization as Evidence to Persuade Management to Allocate More Project Resources?

First, Franklin broke the project down by phase and then by trade, as shown in Figures 8.9 and 8.10. The Pre-Functional Testing was nearly complete, but many integrated tests were still necessary before the building could be finished. Integrated testing refers to testing the interconnection between systems, to ensure they are communicating correctly with each other. When this information was viewed by trade (see Figure 8.10), it became clear that Envelope and Conveyance systems' work had been fully tested, whereas Electrical and Communications systems were the furthest from completion.

Using these two charts, Franklin can, at a glance, see what areas need the most attention, and highlight for management the trades that need additional support. Management can see that a majority of the systems have been installed and verified (Pre-Functional Testing), that verifying the operation of systems is the current focus of efforts (Functional Performance Testing), and that a large amount of systems integration remains to be completed and verified (Integrated Systems Testing).

However, just because the testing of a particular system is complete, does not mean that everything is working correctly. In commissioning, one of the most important tasks is to create and maintain a log of issues noting where the installation **did not** comply with the project design during each test. These deficiency items could be anything from piping installed incorrectly, the wrong window installed, telephones not receiving a dial tone, to the elevator failing to recall on a fire alarm condition. A large number of deficiencies indicates that there are many

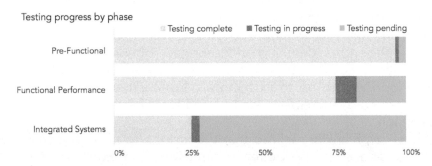

Figure 8.9 Note that the major effort now is in Functional Performance Testing. Franklin is showing how much work remains, using green shading as a preattentive attribute to focus his manager's attention on the pending work.

Testing progress by trade

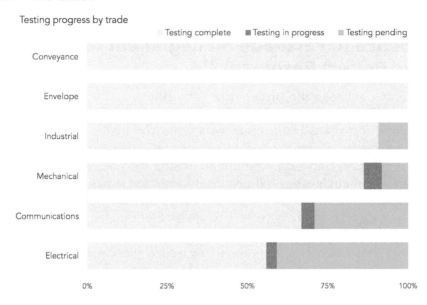

Figure 8.10 This view is a different perspective on the same material. Rather than showing overall phase, Franklin shows which trades have the most work remaining, and therefore where the project managers should focus their efforts.

remaining problems with the project, and that a lot of corrective work needs to be done.

Franklin had been recording, tracking, and closing all of these issues over the past year, so his log had grown quite large. Franklin wanted to show the overall status of issues broken down by whether they were still open or had been closed. This is important information that shows managers a summary of the proportion of problems that remain to be addressed. The pie chart in Figure 8.11 shows, at a glance, that slightly more than half of the deficiencies have been corrected—work has been completed but much work remains to be done!

Primarily, Franklin wanted to show the overall progress. There were 3,217 deficiencies identified on the project. However, the contractors had made a lot of recent effort in fixing the problems. Yet, there was still a long way to go to fix them all. 1,642 issues had been identified, corrected, and closed, while 1,575 remained open and pending resolution.

However, Franklin realized that the insight from the pie chart was obvious and could be better communicated in words than a data graphic. Instead, of showing that a large number of issues had been identified, he decided it was more important to show how many had been corrected. Franklin felt that an area chart would add more context

Percent of open and closed issues

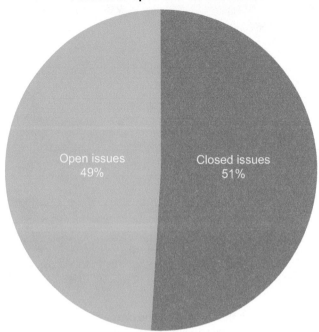

Figure 8.11 The pie chart can quickly show which proportion of the total issues are still open, and therefore need attention.

to the deficiencies because it could include a timeline and show volume of open and closed issues over time. He thought the timeline of the number of issues would show how corrective actions had accelerated recently. Using the area chart, it was clear that the generation rate of issues (corresponding to an increase in the rate of testing) had started increasing in April, and that the contractors had increased the amount of effort in closing issues out since June (see Figure 8.12).

With 49% of the deficiencies remaining open, Franklin wanted to show how many open issues each contractor was responsible for. In particular, Franklin wanted to highlight Penta because it had the most issues left to fix. He decided to group Riptide, Tectric, and Elliot together, since their remaining open issues were a small part of the total.

Finally, Franklin wanted to show the origin of these issues. Were they mostly installation problems, or were systems not communicating with each other? The final chart (see Figure 8.13, Chart B) showed the percentage of deficiencies generated in each phase of testing. Given that Pre-Functional Testing was substantially more complete than the

Number of issues since commissioning start

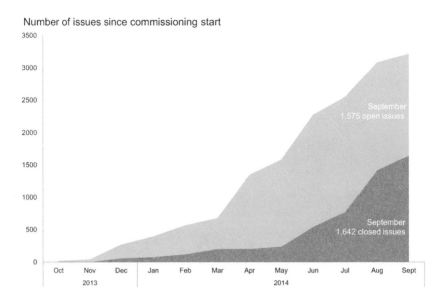

Figure 8.12 The area chart shows not only the proportion of open and closed issues, but it also gives some context by showing the progress over time. It is easy to see that issues were being addressed more rapidly in recent months.

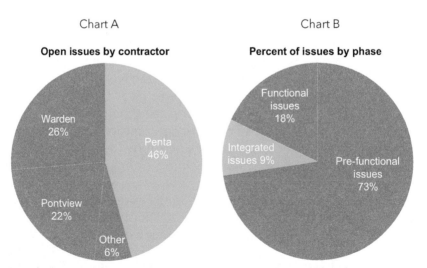

Figure 8.13 Penta has the most open issues, so Franklin highlighted them to draw attention to this in Chart A. Chart B shows that integrated issues comprise a notable portion of the total.

other phases, it was logical to assume that most deficiencies had been generated from this testing. He also wanted to highlight Integrated Systems Testing for special attention. It was still in the early phases, yet there were already a large number of issues being identified. He wanted to make sure his supervisors were aware of this.

As Franklin put the finishing touches on his report, he started thinking of ways to make his reporting more efficient. Why spend hours putting together a custom report every month? What if someone wanted to see the progress on a weekly basis instead? He decided that a web-based dashboard would be a good way to share this information on an ongoing basis with his managers.

Moreover, all the data could fit on a single view and allow managers to dig further into the data to find more details such as which of Penta's open issues were from Pre-Functional Testing. He looked forward to presenting this dashboard at the next team meeting.

Summary

The case presented is an example of using data visualization to report on past data to inform future decision making, project management, and communication. The visualizations were created in Excel and have been modified by the author from their original format for purposes of this publication to better reflect visualization techniques.

Identifying gaming behavior through analytics

Harry Chernoff

This case exemplifies how data graphics highlight categories of casino guests based on which games they play and how much they wager. This knowledge will allow casino managers to decide which games to offer and the level of complimentary items ("comps") to offer their guests. Examples of "comps" include a free All-You-Can-Eat lunch, $150 show tickets, or a private jet ride to the casino.

Introduction

Spanish Trails Casinos (STC) is a leading provider of gaming and entertainment in Las Vegas, Nevada. STC earned the loyalty of its customers by consistently delivering a friendly and fair gaming experience. Part of its popularity comes from its policy of treating its players well, including comps that encourage guests to return more frequently and play longer.

Like most companies in the gaming industry, past business decisions were primarily based on the managements' years of experience and intuition. Historically, almost all executives in the Las Vegas gaming industry were promoted through the ranks; they rose from dealers and pit bosses to managers. Over the past decade, however, the C-Suite executives of the top casinos are of a different character. The current owners are B-school graduates who value modern business analytics. STC recognized the need to develop an evidence-based, data-driven, decision-making culture. This is particularly important to the STC brand, which includes over 20 properties, each with a set of services and amenities including hotel, casino, restaurants, bars, clubs, and spas. Each of STC's businesses yield a rich array of data on customers, marketing effectiveness, purchasing history, supplier sources, human resources, and the industry gaming data.

Historically, each business unit stored and managed its own data for different revenue sources such as slot machines, blackjack tables, and food and liquor sales. Except during regular management meetings, there was little cross-pollination of promotional ideas. When management was interested in the effect of a new marketing campaign, it sampled customers through questionnaires. Analyses of these small data sources were relatively simple to conduct and interpret. However, inferences were prone to error. For example, when the marketing department ran a campaign with half-priced drinks of a particular brand at the bars, it was constrained to work with bar sales data that, although effective for that area, lacked the information about how this affected slot game play at the bar.

In recent years, the diverse data sources are no longer siloed and are accessible by all departments within STC. With the introduction of "Metro Pass" membership cards, STC is learning more about its customers. Now, when guests enter the property, they swipe their cards at the valet service desk for free parking. As they play slot machines, they insert their cards to gain points convertible to gambling dollars. Even the locations where they have lunch are recorded. These actions are tracked for hundreds of thousands of guests on a minute-by-minute basis. However, this has created additional challenges for STC; it needs to rethink how it stores, interprets, and mines this data to maximize what it can learn about its customers' behaviors and patterns.

For all of the gambling sources on the floor, STC executives monitor the performance of each machine or game type over time. The key metric has been the revenue per game as shown in Figure 8.14.

STC also compares the performance of games of the same type at different locations within the property, or at other properties. Table 8.7 shows the top ranking games and the square footage allotted for each game located within one of STC's properties.

The Bingo Dilemma

STC knows a lot about its customers, especially its Bingo players. The Bingo Room is an institution in STC properties, tracing back to the first casinos that were opened. The Bingo clientele is generally older adults, averaging over 70 years of age. Each Bingo game takes on average approximately 40 minutes to complete. Since the players are mostly elderly, rushing the games along is not consistent with STC policy of friendly, attentive service. However, Bingo is not a game that is very profitable for the casino. So, why do they have it at all? It has become one of the trademarks of STC. However, current management is less convinced that STC's rather large Bingo parlor (over 24,000 square feet), which seriously cuts into the profitable square footage on the casino floor, should be continued for only nostalgic reasons.

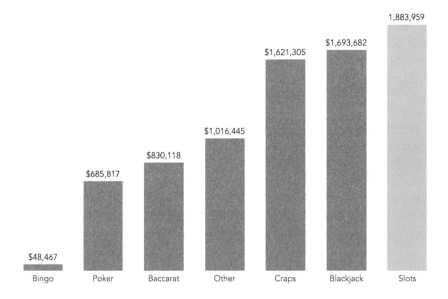

Revenue per game over a 24-hour period

						1,883,959
					$1,693,682	
				$1,621,305		
			$1,016,445			
	$830,118					
$685,817						
$48,467						
Bingo	Poker	Baccarat	Other	Craps	Blackjack	Slots

Figure 8.14 Spanish Trails Casino—revenue by game over a 24-hour period

Table 8.7 Casino floor space by game

Gaming Area	Square Footage	% of Floor
Slot Floor	113,690	55.10%
Table Games (Craps & Blackjack)	9,955	4.80%
Table Games (Other)	2,489	1.20%
Keno	2,725	1.30%
Bingo	24,016	11.60%
Poker Room	6,229	3.00%
Race & Sports	19,203	9.30%
Other Gaming Areas	28,100	13.60%
Total	206,406	100%

Rankings based on revenue	Rankings based on profitability
1. Slots	1. Slots
2. Blackjack & Craps	2. Blackjack & Craps
3. Other Table Games	3. Other Table Games
4. Poker	4. Poker
5. Bingo	5. Bingo

Maintaining Customers' Loyalty

Customer relations have major implications for the casino's results. For instance, the directors of the slot machines use analytics to identify frequent guests and high-value players who are on the floor. They can notify team members to follow up with personal greetings and comps. STC's "Metro Pass" Player Rewards Program, facilitated by complex gaming industry technology, alerts managers to these real-time opportunities. To keep a constant flow of this type of data coming in, customers are given incentives to sign up for, and use, their customer rewards cards. Customers earn points for slot and table game play at any of the (STC) properties and can redeem them for gambling play, merchandise, food, lodging, movie passes, child care, and concert tickets. This incentivizes customers to use their reward cards to record their play. The data collected includes which games were played, the start and end time of each play, and their monetary results. Management strives to acquire information that could result in a competitive advantage. For example, what different types of comps should be offered to the varied categories of players?

Challenge for the Consulting Team

STC outsourced a small consulting team to provide data to help it answer two major questions:

1. Should STC close down the Bingo room?
2. How does STC determine what to comp its casino guests?

Question 1: The Bingo Decision

The casino shared a snapshot of data with the consulting group. This data was a summary of the most recent 24-hour period. This included the betting data of the most recent 5,000 players, broken down by game and amount wagered. Table 8.8 presents an excerpt of this data.

The consulting team began its work. The team could easily see revenue per game (previously presented in Figure 8.14), but it did not know the range of dollars bet in the Bingo room compared to the other games. The team reported with a simple series of boxplots (see Figure 8.15. The boxplots show the breakdown of dollars played by player over a 24-hour period, by game. Each player is represented by a green dot on the boxplot. Boxplots are effective at showing the median value and the range of values. It was clear that the majority of

Table 8.8 A snapshot of the daily game play data by player

Player ID	Slots	Blackjack	Craps	Baccarat	Bingo	Poker	Other	Total Spend
Player 1	0	0	0	1037	0	1353	483	2874
Player 2	357	0	0	0	23	0	0	380
Player 3	565	209	93	0	0	723	272	1861
Player 4	0	869	183	0	0	465	723	2240
Player 5	0	0	0	0	0	0	0	0
Player 6	0	0	885	0	0	0	0	885
Player 7	283	0	0	0	0	0	0	283
Player 8	41	205	0	133	0	195	1311	1885
Player 9	1208	216	775	212	0	0	138	2548
Player 10	560	0	0	0	0	0	0	560

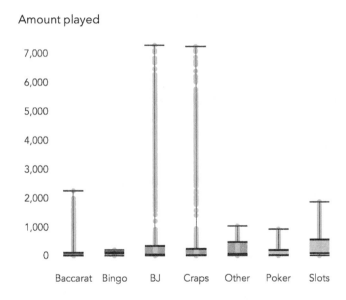

Figure 8.15 A boxplot for each of the seven games analyzed by the consultants

the spend per game was under $1,000, as shown by the gray boxes. High spenders who played upwards of $7,000 on a single game was only evident in Blackjack and Craps play.

The consultants developed an interactive dashboard to filter by game to provide more detail on the Bingo players (see Figure 8.16). The total amount spent on Bingo over a 24-hour period was $48,467. Most players bet an average of $98. A total of 494 out of 5,000

Amount played

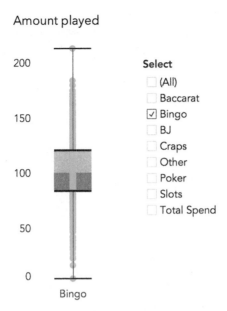

Figure 8.16 A dashboard that shows a boxplot highlighting the amount played on Bingo by 494 customers over the last 24 hours

customers played Bingo, with a total spend between $5 and $213. This is less than 10% of total customers. These players account for only 6% of STC's total revenue of $7,779,802.

It was clear from this data that the revenue from Bingo was small relative to any of the other games the casino offered. Based on this information alone, it would have been an easy decision to close the Bingo parlor down.

But there was other data to examine, such as the playing patterns of the Bingo enthusiasts. The consultants sought to reexamine the data along this line of inquiry: are the Bingo customers playing a combination of Bingo and other games? The answer to this question would determine if Bingo players were really a separate group that could be cut off with little revenue loss.

The analysts used a simple scatterplot matrix to quickly analyze and show the relationships between dollars played by every game to each other game (see Figure 8.17).

The scatterplot makes it immediately apparent that some Bingo players also play the slot machines. This is evident in the second column and the last row in the scatterplot matrix. In fact, the only other game Bingo customers play is slot machines. There was more involved here than simply losing the Bingo business. If the Bingo parlor was

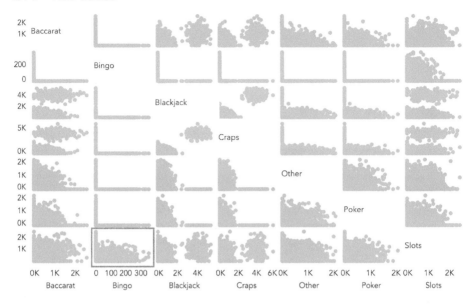

Figure 8.17 A scatterplot matrix that plots relationship between every variable (game) to each other–Bingo and slots are highlighted with a gray box

eliminated, would STC also lose this slot business because players went to other Bingo venues? Very possibly and. if so, the loss would be over $200,000 per day.

The importance of this knowledge highlighted one of the major advantages of innovative business analytics practices, which is to look at the all of the information across departments (in this case, games).

Question 2: Incentivizing Customers Through Complimentary Items and Services to Encourage Players to Gamble

In the past, the managers had always provided complimentary items and services to their customers to encourage them to gamble. The process was subjective, and often the managers were guessing at what to give their customers to motivate them to play longer and return more frequently. One thing was clear, different players were playing very different amounts, and they needed to distinguish the slot player who gambled $30 or $40 per day on a nickel or quarter machine, from the high rollers who played $5 to $10 per spin, adding up to thousands of dollars per day.

The analysts decided to mine the betting data further to determine if there were distinct groups or categories of players, and if they could be profiled. The consultants used a clustering technique[10] to analyze the data. After numerous runs of the model, certain classifications and categories emerged, as shown in a revised scatterplot matrix (see Figure 8.18). Each color represented a different cluster or category. Now the data could be viewed in terms of those players who have similar spending, by game, across all games. Each dot represents a player and each color represents a cluster.

The differences in each cluster are shown in Table 8.9. This shows the average amount played per game and the average total spent by cluster.

The cluster analysis was run multiple times changing the number of clusters (or groupings) from two to six. Each of these analyses were studied to determine absolute differences between the clusters.

Cluster analysis of daily spend by game and player

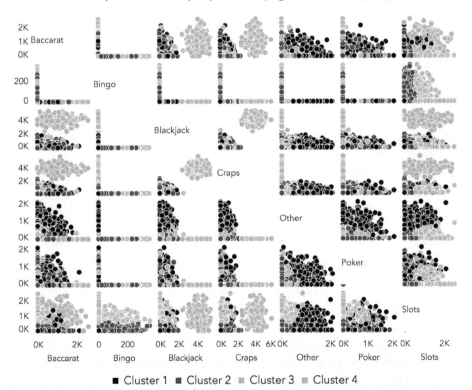

■ Cluster 1 ■ Cluster 2 ■ Cluster 3 ■ Cluster 4

Figure 8.18 A scatterplot matrix that plots relationship between every variable (game) to each other and colored by cluster

Table 8.9 The result of the cluster analysis that shows four clusters, highlighting four different play types based on average play patterns and total spent

Cluster	Number of players	Baccarat	Bingo	Blackjack	Craps	Poker	Other	Slots	Average Total Spent
1	842	255.89	0.00	276.51	261.27	329.76	853.70	424.28	2,401.40
2	2850	81.88	10.58	116.12	102.97	95.88	61.56	109.70	578.71
3	1076	121.11	17.00	181.26	174.45	125.37	113.54	916.98	1,656.70
4	232	1,049.30	0.00	4,029.70	3,966.10	0.0	0.00	980.16	10,025.00

Where the differences are greater, the groups are more distinct from one another, and the cluster can be managed with unique strategies and marketing techniques. It was determined that the analysis with four clusters resulted in the best differentiation among all of the casino guests.

From these results, it was possible for management to define the characteristics of each category (betting group). The following four groups were identified:

Comping Results

It was important for the casino to estimate a short- and long-term value of a customer. This was done by combining the dollar size of the game played, the amount the player spent, how long the player stayed on the floor, and how often the player returned to the casino. The results of the data mining and cluster analysis added much accuracy and reliability to the grouping of casino's players.

The proper comp for each of these groups was determined by matching proportionate rewards to each group identified in Table 8.10. The comp for a slots player might be between $5 and $20 in free slots play. This would just show up on the machine when the player sat down and inserted their card. Other, more valued players, received invitations at their homes to take advantage of a free weekend at the casino. The very high rollers were contacted personally by player representatives.

These policies were tested and refined over time, with more data, and adjusted accordingly.

Table 8.10 Classification of players into four distinct categories

Category or cluster		Gambling behavior
1	Compulsive	Plays every game on the casino floor, moving around constantly. Their action is divided evenly over all games (excluding Bingo). Has difficulty walking past any table without playing it. Most play is on slots. This group spends an average of $2500 per day on the casino floor.
2	Small Bettor (Grandma)	These players are small bettors, most averaging under $100 per day. The group includes the small Slot machine players (nickel or quarter slots) and Bingo players.
3	Slot Players	These players primarily play the Slot machines, but are more aggressive bettors (than category 2), often reaching over $1000 per day in total spend.
4	High Roller	Experienced gamblers who play the best games (best odds for the player) and average about $10,000 of play per day. Their average action is spread over, at best, four games (Slots (10%); Blackjack (40%); Craps (40%); Baccarat (10%).

Summary

Using data visualizations to show which casino games people play, and how much they wager per day, is a tool that exposes casino gambling patterns and can be of ultimate importance to the casino owners. The casino decision makers want to know what kind of a player you are and what your lifetime value is to them before they start "comping" you and enticing you to return.

Exploring the openings and closings of NYC schools

Reshama Shaikh and Riyaz Shaikh

Creating interactive data graphics enables others to explore data for themselves, and allows for the presentation of rich information that can be filtered, magnified, and used to compare changes over time through animation. This project was created and presented in December 2013 in collaboration with NYU Stern School of Business and The Research Alliance for New York City Schools.

Introduction

The NYC school system is the largest in the United States and probably the largest in the world. The Research Alliance for New York City Schools (RANYCS) conducts rigorous studies on topics that matter to the city's public schools. Its recent studies of school systems often work in percentages, or discuss an analysis based on a small subset of students in NYC schools. This can make it easy to lose sight of the scale and scope of RANYCS's research. We worked with RANYCS to explore how to "put their work in context" to illustrate to its diverse audience (teachers, parents, students, educators, other school systems, researchers, and policy makers).

Our project uses a web-based map to display the changes in the density of NYC schools over time. To explore these changes, we needed data on school enrollment, school location, and school functioning status (such as new, open, or closed). These data were sourced from RANYCS, spanning a period of 17 years from 1996 to 2012.

We sought to answer the following questions about NYC high schools:

- How is the enrollment by school district fluctuating over time?
- Where are the high schools' opening and closing or staying statics?

How Is Enrollment Changing by District Over Time?

A filled-map was used to show distribution of enrollment across school districts and allow comparisons among districts. Lighter shaded districts indicate fewer students per school, while darker shaded districts indicate highly populated schools. The data graphics in Table 8.11 present a time lapse of which districts were in urgent need of more schools, while also drawing attention to nearby districts that might be able to serve more students.

For example, in 1996, the Bronx had low student enrollment (see Figure 8.19). The neighboring districts (with areas shaded darker) faced a different problem; their schools were very populated. Using the web-based version of this map, when a user hovers over a district, a sparkline shows the change in student enrollments over time. In the case of district 9, the enrollment was 191 in 1996. The sparkline shows the growth in enrollment since 1996.

For more detail on the exact location of each NYC school and enrollment size, we created an alternative view of this information. We used a time lapse bubble map (see Table 8.12). The size of each bubble is proportional to the school's enrollment for that year. In most districts outside of Manhattan, there were few large schools. However, Manhattan had a mix of small and large schools. The web-based time-lapse animation shows how some schools grew, while others shrunk over time.

Table 8.11 A filled map that shows the average student enrollment by school district over time

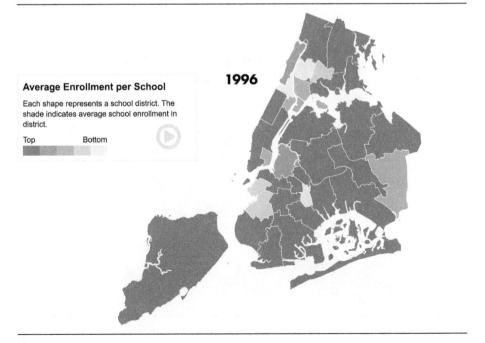

(Continued)

Table 8.11 (Continued)

Average Enrollment per School

Each shape represents a school district. The shade indicates average school enrollment in district.

Top   Bottom

1997

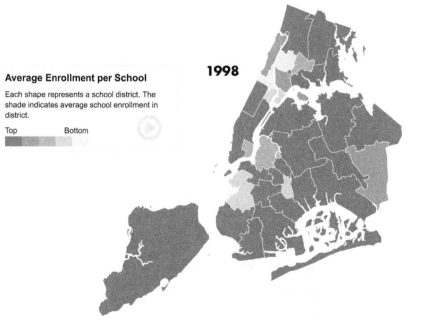

Average Enrollment per School

Each shape represents a school district. The shade indicates average school enrollment in district.

Top   Bottom

1998

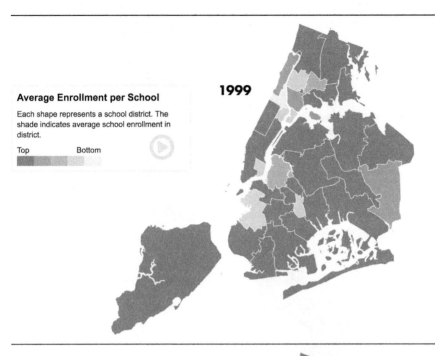

Average Enrollment per School

Each shape represents a school district. The shade indicates average school enrollment in district.

Top   Bottom

1999

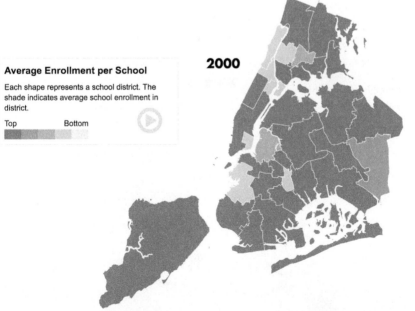

Average Enrollment per School

Each shape represents a school district. The shade indicates average school enrollment in district.

Top   Bottom

2000

(Continued)

Table 8.11 (Continued)

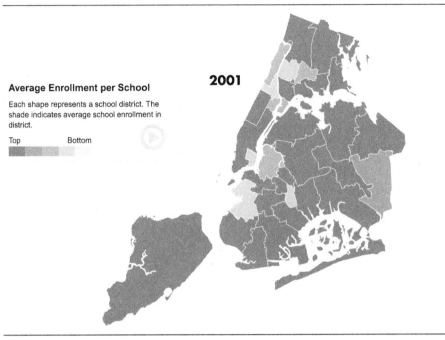

Average Enrollment per School

Each shape represents a school district. The shade indicates average school enrollment in district.

Top   Bottom

2001

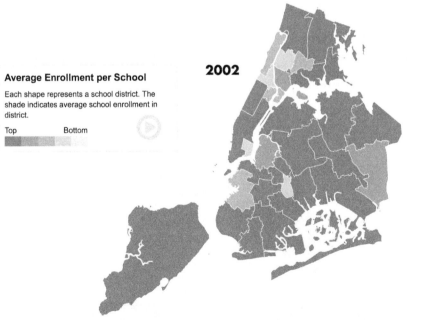

Average Enrollment per School

Each shape represents a school district. The shade indicates average school enrollment in district.

Top   Bottom

2002

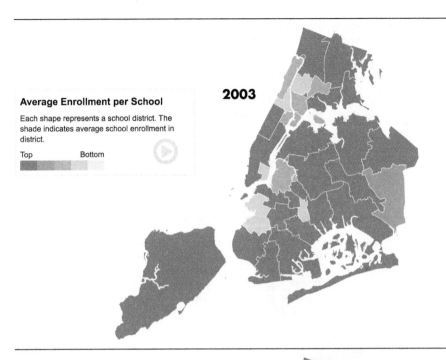

2003

Average Enrollment per School

Each shape represents a school district. The shade indicates average school enrollment in district.

Top   Bottom

2004

Average Enrollment per School

Each shape represents a school district. The shade indicates average school enrollment in district.

Top   Bottom

(Continued)

Table 8.11 (Continued)

Average Enrollment per School

Each shape represents a school district. The shade indicates average school enrollment in district.

Top   Bottom

2005

Average Enrollment per School

Each shape represents a school district. The shade indicates average school enrollment in district.

Top   Bottom

2006

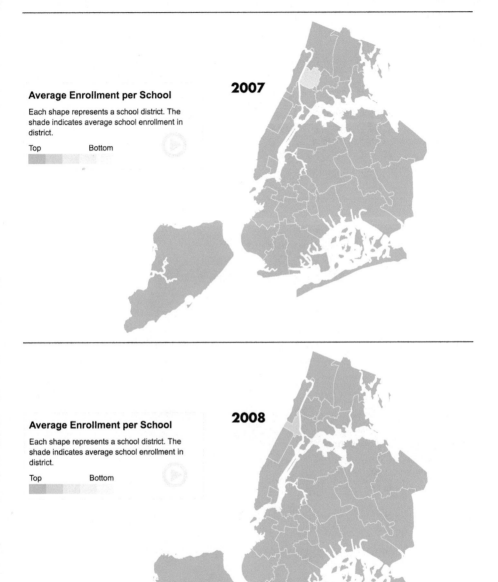

Average Enrollment per School

Each shape represents a school district. The
shade indicates average school enrollment in
district.

Top   Bottom

2007

Average Enrollment per School

Each shape represents a school district. The
shade indicates average school enrollment in
district.

Top   Bottom

2008

(Continued)

Table 8.11 (Continued)

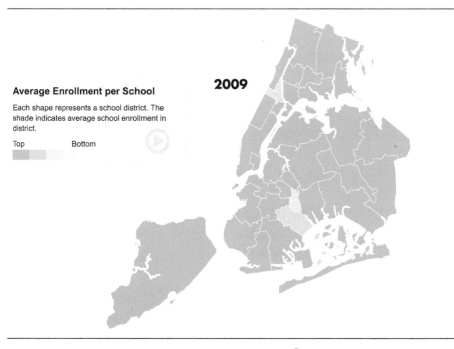

Average Enrollment per School

Each shape represents a school district. The shade indicates average school enrollment in district.

Top   Bottom

2009

Average Enrollment per School

Each shape represents a school district. The shade indicates average school enrollment in district.

Top   Bottom

2010

Average Enrollment per School

Each shape represents a school district. The shade indicates average school enrollment in district.

Top   Bottom

2011

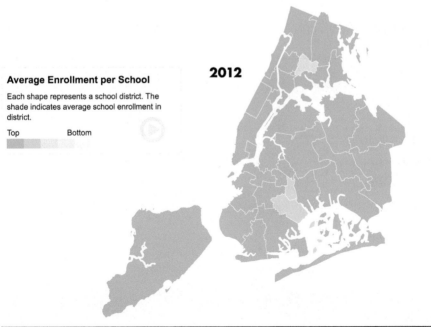

Average Enrollment per School

Each shape represents a school district. The shade indicates average school enrollment in district.

Top   Bottom

2012

(Continued)

Average Enrollment per School

Each shape represents a school district. The shade indicates average school enrollment in district.

Top   Bottom

1996

District 9
Average Enrolled: 191

1996

Figure 8.19 The average student enrollment by district with district 9 highlighted

Table 8.12 A time lapse of NYC schools from 1996 through 2012 with bubbles sized by student enrollment

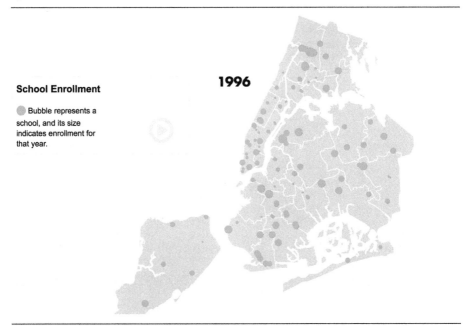

School Enrollment

Bubble represents a school, and its size indicates enrollment for that year.

1996

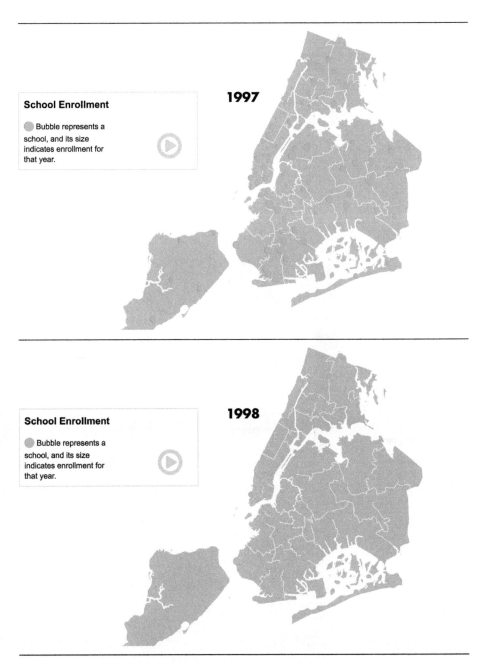

School Enrollment

Bubble represents a school, and its size indicates enrollment for that year.

1997

School Enrollment

Bubble represents a school, and its size indicates enrollment for that year.

1998

(Continued)

Table 8.12 (Continued)

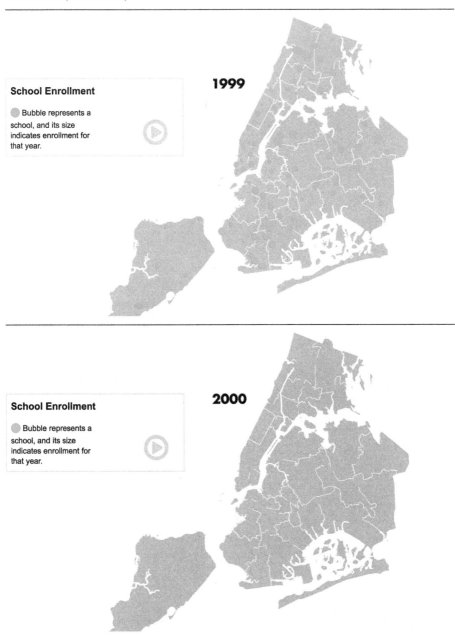

School Enrollment

Bubble represents a school, and its size indicates enrollment for that year.

1999

School Enrollment

Bubble represents a school, and its size indicates enrollment for that year.

2000

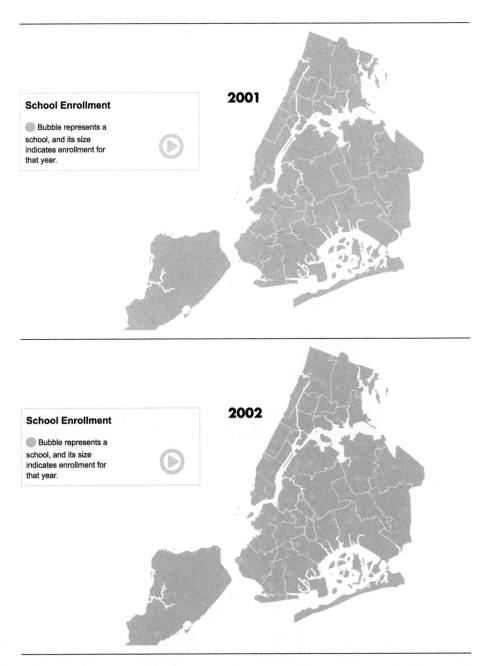

(Continued)

Table 8.12 (Continued)

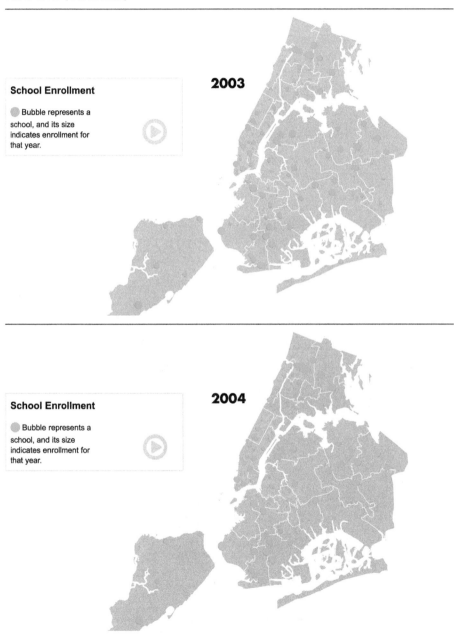

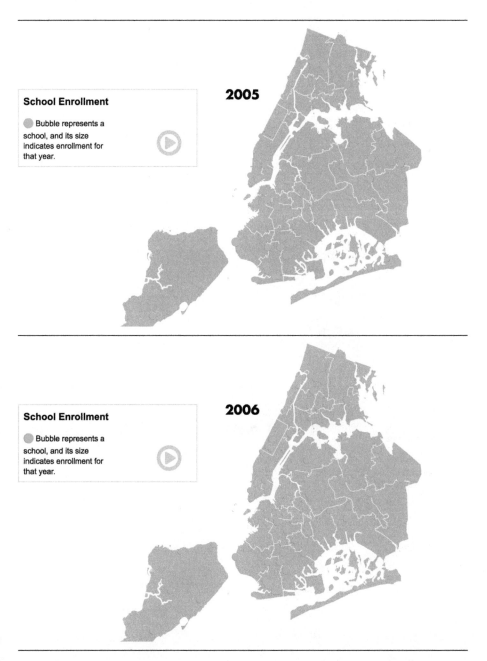

(Continued)

Table 8.12 (Continued)

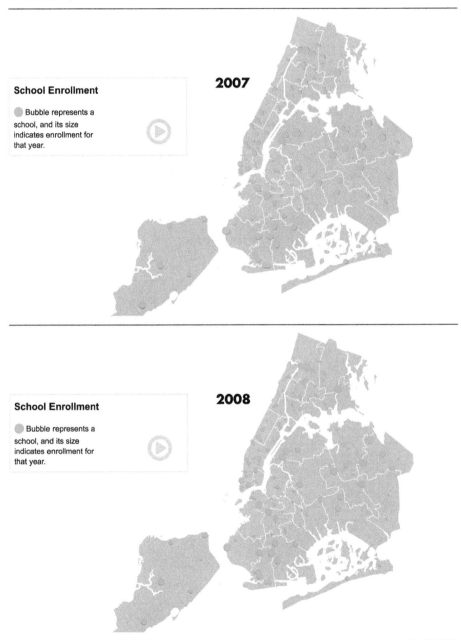

School Enrollment

Bubble represents a school, and its size indicates enrollment for that year.

2007

School Enrollment

Bubble represents a school, and its size indicates enrollment for that year.

2008

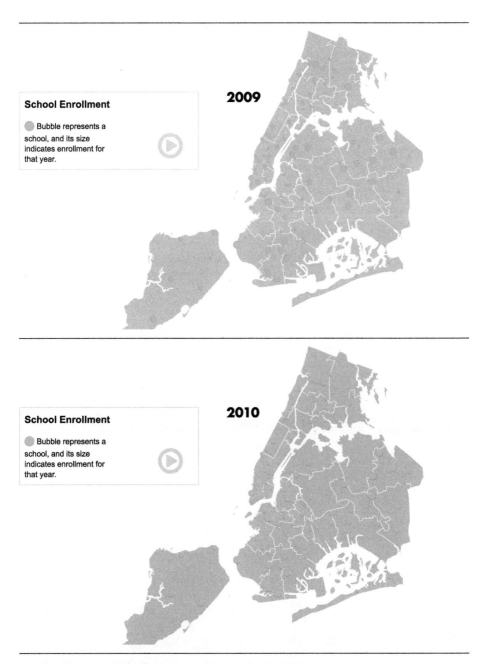

(Continued)

Table 8.12 (Continued)

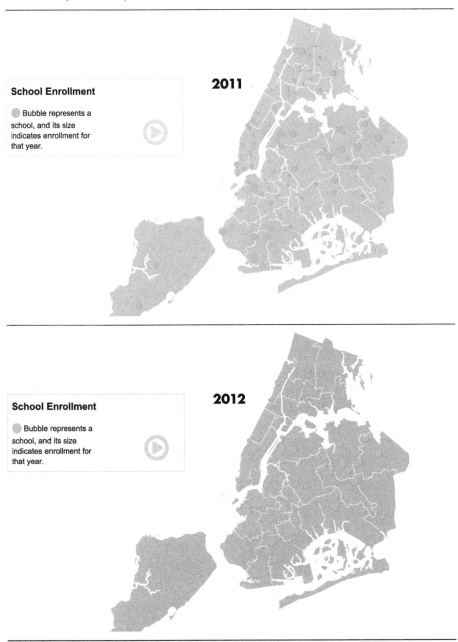

School Enrollment

Bubble represents a
school, and its size
indicates enrollment for
that year.

2011

School Enrollment

Bubble represents a
school, and its size
indicates enrollment for
that year.

2012

How Is Enrollment Changing by School Over Time?

The charts in Table 8.12 are interactive; users hover over either a district or school to reveal more detail that includes the total number of students enrolled for the year selected and a sparkline that shows the changes in enrollment from 1996 through 2012. See Table 8.13.

Table 8.13 Two bubble maps that show student enrollment by school and district for 2012

School enrollment shown by district

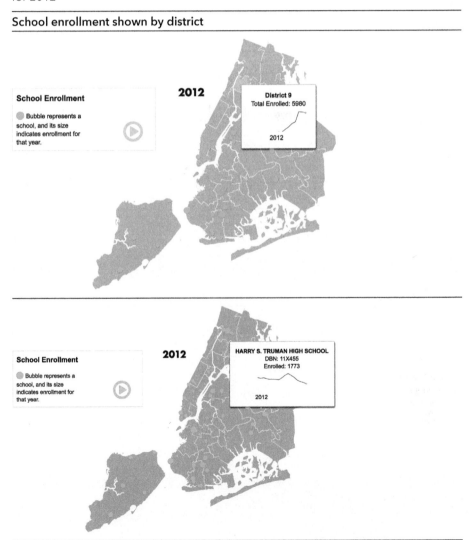

Where Have New Schools Opened? Where Have Schools Closed?

Based on student enrollments by school and district, the number of schools, student demand, and a number of other factors have led to the opening of new schools and the closing of others.

We wanted to map these changes in school openings and closings over time. Table 8.14 shows, for a given time period, existing schools, new schools that opened, and the schools that have closed. Bold colors were used to draw attention to closings. Animation was used to show the pace of openings and closings over time.

Table 8.14 The location of school openings and closings by district in NYC

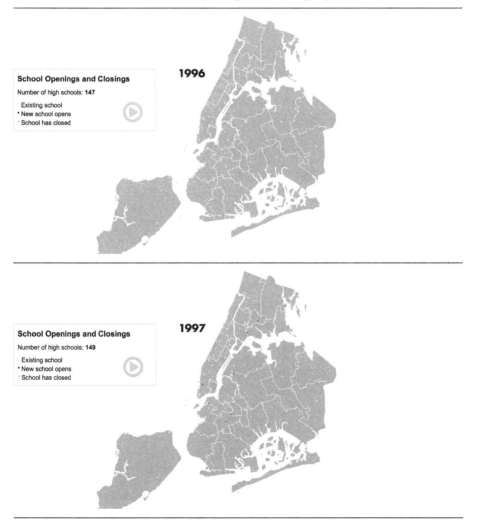

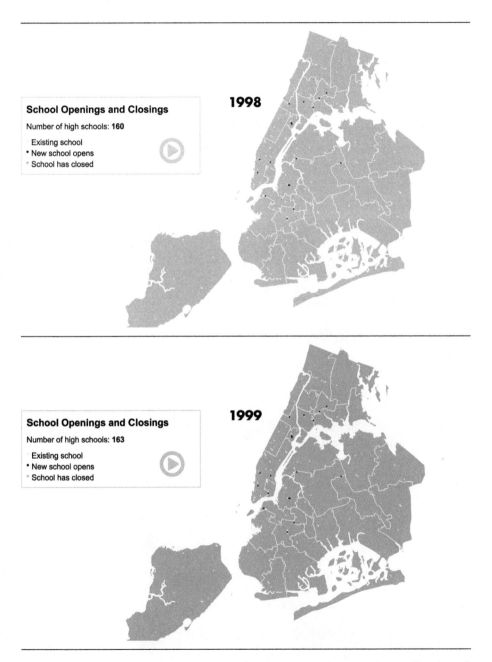

(Continued)

Table 8.14 (Continued)

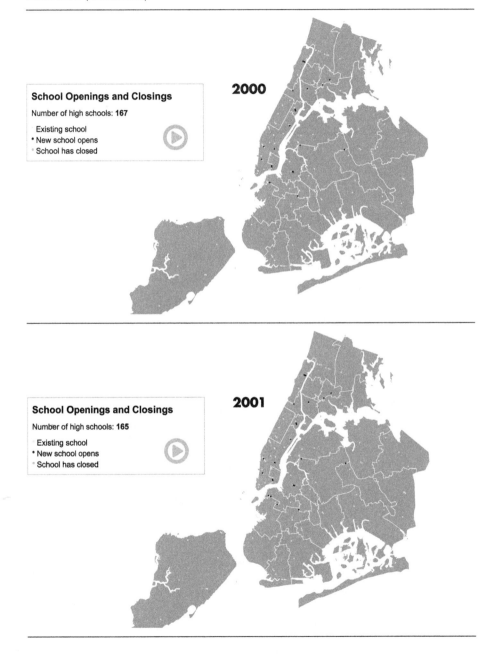

School Openings and Closings

Number of high schools: **167**

Existing school
* New school opens
° School has closed

2000

School Openings and Closings

Number of high schools: **165**

Existing school
* New school opens
° School has closed

2001

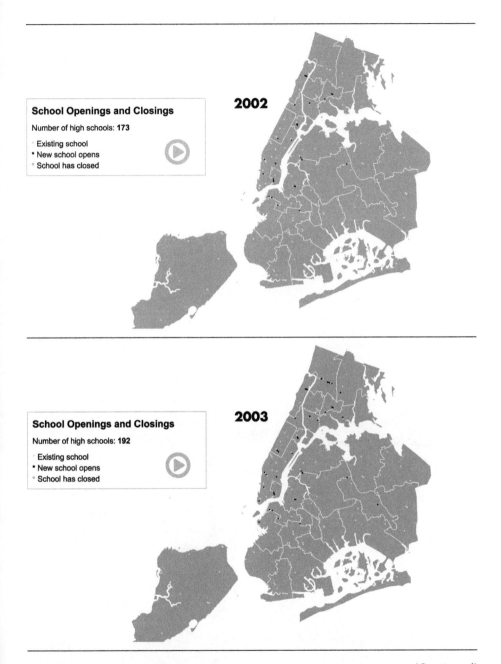

School Openings and Closings

Number of high schools: **173**

- Existing school
- New school opens
- School has closed

2002

School Openings and Closings

Number of high schools: **192**

- Existing school
- New school opens
- School has closed

2003

(Continued)

Table 8.14 (Continued)

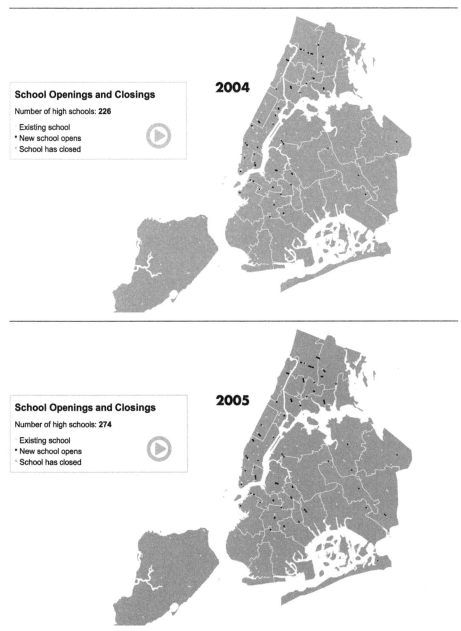

School Openings and Closings

Number of high schools: **226**

Existing school
* New school opens
° School has closed

2004

School Openings and Closings

Number of high schools: **274**

Existing school
* New school opens
° School has closed

2005

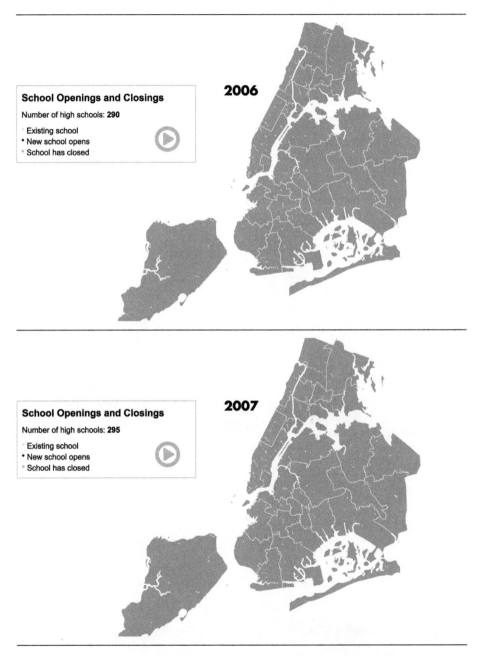

School Openings and Closings

Number of high schools: **290**

- Existing school
- New school opens
- School has closed

2006

School Openings and Closings

Number of high schools: **295**

- Existing school
- New school opens
- School has closed

2007

(Continued)

Table 8.14 (Continued)

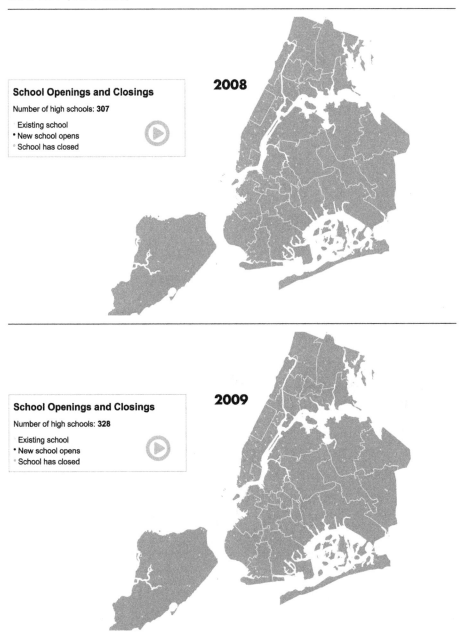

School Openings and Closings

Number of high schools: **307**

 Existing school
• New school opens
 School has closed

2008

School Openings and Closings

Number of high schools: **328**

 Existing school
• New school opens
 School has closed

2009

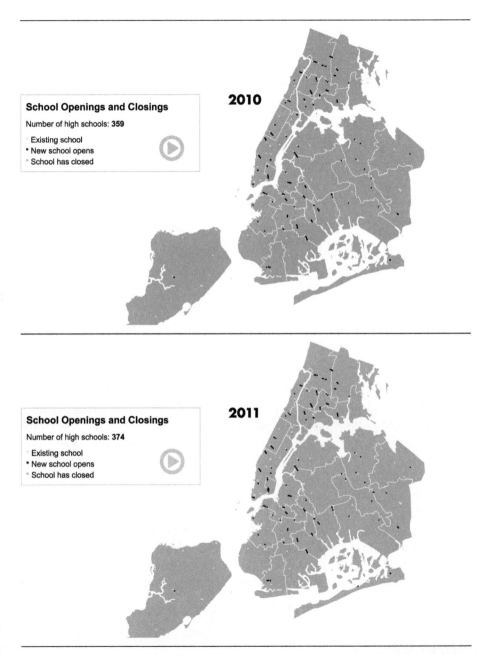

(Continued)

Table 8.14 (Continued)

Summary

From this exploratory investigation into NYC schools, we learned that the NYC school system is dynamic; some districts are growing with more schools while others are shrinking. From 1996 to 2012, the number of high schools in NYC increased while average enrollment per school decreased. This change was most pronounced beginning in 2002. While there are many reasons for these changes, we learned that dropout rates increased in all five boroughs (7% in 1996 to 12% in 2012). This finding one of many for this type of exploratory study.

The case presented is an example of using data graphics as an interface for information exploration. It is a web-based visualization using the D3 JavaScript framework. It allows for zooming, panning, and time series animation. Interact with it at: http://becomingvisual.com/portfolio/nycschools

Wrap Up

These five cases represent a diverse use of data graphics. From exploratory research to presenting results, the cases were intended to show different methods for analyzing data and presenting findings.

With each case, the audience, task (intent), data, and the accompanying data graphics were presented.[11] In your work, define your audience, task, data, and data graphics to document your data stories as you continue to practice becoming visual.

Notes

1 Rojas, Fabio. 'How Twitter Can Predict an Election.' *The Washington Post*. August 11, 2013, para 1-3. www.washingtonpost.com/opinions/how-twitter-can-predict-an-election/2013/08/11/35ef885a-0108-11e3-96a8-d3b921c0924a_story.html?utm_term=.010d90e6bdfa

2 Furnas, Alexander. 'You Can't Use Twitter To Predict Election Results.' *The Atlantic*. May 15, 2012. www.theatlantic.com/technology/archive/2012/05/you-cant-use-twitter-to-predict-election-results/257201/

3 Roose, Kevin. 'Political Donors Put Their Money Where the Memes Are.' *The New York Times*. Page B1. August 7, 2017.

4 Bavel, Jay Van. 'Twitter's Passion Politics.' *The New York Times*. Page SR8. July 9, 2017.

5 "2016 NVCA Yearbook," sourced from http://nvca.org/pressreleases/2016-nvca-yearbook-captures-busy-year-for-venture-capital-activity/. Number of new companies formed, sourced from Bureau of Labor Statistics, available at www.bls.gov/bdm/entrepreneurship/bdm_chart1.htm

6 Aingel Corp. is a firm that studies the startup ecosystem. It has developed a proprietary artificial intelligence algorithm to identify indicators of team performance as predictors of team success. Examples of indicators include educational details, work history, entrepreneurial activity, personality scores, and hundreds of other variables.

7 www.endurecap.com/

8 Haislip, A. (2011). *Essentials of Venture Capital*. Hoboken, NJ: Wiley. Page 106.

9 This case was written to illustrate a commonplace scenario faced by a construction manager. The situation is based on real life, but the names of the characters and companies presented are fictional to preserve confidentiality.

10 The consultants used a k-means method to mine the data. A k-means clustering partitions the observations into clusters (specifically, k clusters). Each observation belongs to the cluster with the nearest mean.

11 I learned this framework from Hanspeter Pfister at Harvard University during his workshop on data visualization.

IX

THE
END

Where do we go from here?

9.1 Your Visual Habits

I write this conclusion at the beginning of a new year. We all make New Year's resolutions to change some aspect of our lives for the better.

Developing your visualization habits requires practice. The preceding chapters set a foundation to build and expand your knowledge. I wanted to leave you with four cognitive shortcuts that present the most ubiquitous challenges and how to address them. Following these shortcuts are archetypes or blueprints for the most common types of data graphics. Use the archetypes as templates to create your data graphics style (font face, font size, and color).

1. THE DATA GRAPHIC AUTOMATON

An automaton is "a self-operating machine, or a machine or control mechanism designed to automatically follow a predetermined sequence of operations, or respond to predetermined instructions" (Wikipedia, 2018, para 1).

Challenge: software is powerful, but sometimes we need to verify the data and results. Check the validity of the data encodings and aggregations.

Takeaway: do not be the data graphic automaton. Know what your data means and double check that your calculations are correct.

2. THE PARTY FAVOR

According to Wikipedia, a party favor "is a small gift given to the guests at a party as a gesture of thanks for their attendance, a memento of the occasion, or simply as an aid to frivolity" (2018, para 1).

Challenge: people take time out of their day to attend your presentation. Ensure your audience walks away with something of value.

Takeaway: communicate to your audience the main point or key conclusion that you want them to remember.

3. THE BIG "RED" BUBBLE

Hans Rosling's TED Talk presentation serves as the classic example of how to clearly explain a data graphic to an audience. Watch this video: http://becoming visual.com/portfolio/hansrosling. Rosling explains the axes, the colors, and the encodings. Listen for when he describes China as "the big red bubble" as a cue to point the audience's attention to the country of interest.

Challenge: even if a legend is present, take the time to describe how the data is encoded. For example, what do the lines, points, filled areas, or bubbles mean? Label the units used, whether they be U.S. dollars or Japanese Yen, hours or minutes, kilometers or miles, degrees Fahrenheit or Celsius.

Takeaway: take the time to explain the chart elements to your audience.

4. THE DOLPHIN IN THE ROSE

 A classic optical illusion used to explain elements of human memory and perception is a picture of a rose with a dolphin hidden in the rose's petals. Look at the original image: http://becoming visual.com/portfolio/dolphin.

Use data graphics that clearly and obviously show a trend, a relationship mapped to the chart that is designed to show the particular insight. Your audience is looking for common or familiar patterns. For example, a picture of a dolphin in a rose is not what we expect to see.

Challenge: make the insight easy to spot. Reduce data density. Select a chart type that shows the findings without extraneous explanations.

Takeaway: make sure your insight is not the dolphin hidden in the rose.

9.2 Archetypes

Design your workflow to make it an "easy lift" to incorporate visualization into your practice. Identify the tools and software that make it simple to create brilliant charts, plots, maps, and diagrams.

Create templates or sample charts you can modify for different formats: presentations, the web, and print. These templates will be helpful when you need to create a data graphic in a jiffy.

Below are nine archetypes to help you build your templates. The design standards are applied to each chart. The charts are in grayscale. All of the archetypes available for download at: http://becoming visual.com/portfolio/archetypes

LINE CHART

Figures 9.1 and 9.2 are designed for use with time series data. Use the line chart for up to four data series. The stacked area chart is best for comparing the relative differences between two or more series.

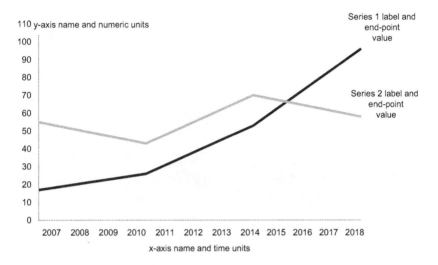

Figure 9.1 An archetype for a basic line chart

STACKED AREA CHART

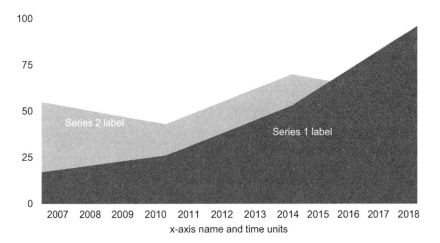

Figure 9.2 An archetype for a stacked area chart

HORIZONTAL BAR CHART

To show rank or ordering, such as the top five employees, use a horizontal chart (Figure 9.3). Order the bars in descending order, from largest to smallest. Label the bars with the data values.

x-axis name and numeric units

Figure 9.3 An archetype for a horizontal bar chart

STACKED COLUMN BAR CHART

For showing subcategories or portions over time or by another categorical variable, use a stacked bar chart (Figure 9.4). Keep the subcategories to four or less. Include a legend that defines the subcategories
by color.

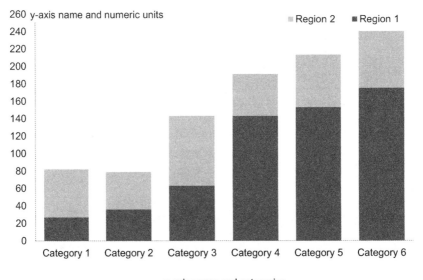

Figure 9.4 An archetype for a stacked vertical bar chart

VERTICAL COLUMN BAR CHART

For comparing two groups within a single category, use a vertical bar chart that shows the comparisons side by side. Figure 9.5 uses two vertical bars per category to show the groups or subcategories, which are distinguished by color. Remove the y-axis and directly label the bars.

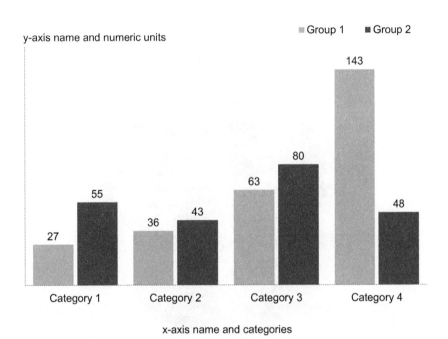

Figure 9.5 An archetype for a basic vertical column bar chart

BASIC PIE

To show a proportion of a whole, a pie chart (or bar chart) works well when there six or less parts that comprise the whole. Figure 9.6 shows a pie chart with the pie slices labeled by percentages, with the total of all slices adding up to 100%. Use the same color for the slices and use whitespace in between the slices to distinguish them from one another. Label with values and the name of the each slice.

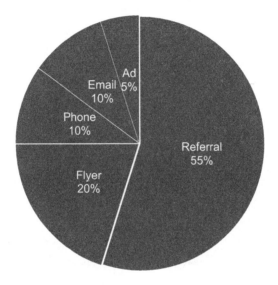

Figure 9.6 An archetype for a pie chart

SCATTERPLOT

For showing relationships between two numeric variables, use a scatterplot. Figure 9.7 is an archetype for a basic scatterplot with a single data point labeled and a linear trend line.

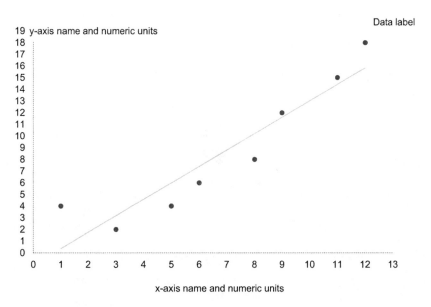

Figure 9.7 An archetype for a scatterplot

BUBBLE CHART

To show relationships between three or more numeric variables, a bubble chart allows for up to four variables to be encoded: position of x and y, and the size and color of the bubble. A legend is useful to explain the meaning of the size and color.

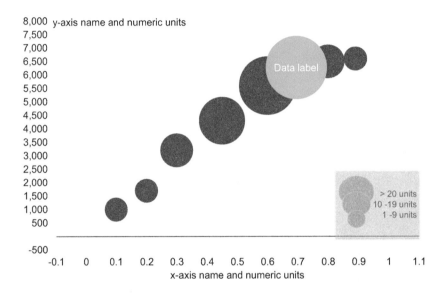

Figure 9.8 An archetype for a bubble chart

BASIC TABLE

Sometimes you just want to show information organized in columns and rows. A table of numbers may be all that is needed. Figure 9.9 shows a simple table that organizes products, cost, price, and profit into a 4 × 5 table. Note the minimum use of gridlines and the alignment of the numeric data.

Product name	Cost	Price	Profit
B10	0.3	4.99	$4.69
B12	0.5	6.99	$6.49
B15	0.7	10.99	$10.29
B20	0.9	15.99	$15.09

Figure 9.9 An archetype for a basic table

Use these archetypes along with the design standards checklist (see Chapter V) to guide you and others in the creation of clear data graphics.

9.3 Keep Visualizing, Keep Learning, and Keep in Touch

Use data graphics as evidence to support your message. Make it easy for your audience to interpret the key insights from your charts. Find ways to connect with your audience through discussion, questions, surveys, and building on their prior knowledge. Remember, you know your data. It's your job to help others understand it. Keep in mind that you are the designer and in complete control of which data is or is not displayed. Share your work with others to "test out" your data graphics and seek feedback. The becomingvisual.com website is a place for you to share your work and practice. As technologies and techniques advance, I will continue to share my practice with you on the book website. I also encourage you to seek out formal training in data visualization software and programming packages. I've created a short list of training opportunities and the top workshops on data visualization at: http://becomingvisual.com/training

Notes

Luis Prado from the Noun Project created the "gift" image used for the party favor explanation.

Creative Stall from the Noun Project created the "mechanical man" image used for the data graphic automaton explanation.

Royyan Razka from the Noun Project created the "bubble" image used for the big red bubble explanation.

Lluis Pareras from the Noun Project created the "rose" image used for the dolphin in the rose explanation.

Bibliography

Automaton. Retrieved from https://en.wikipedia.org/wiki/Automaton on January 1, 2018

Party favor. Retrieved from https://en.wikipedia.org/wiki/Party_favor on January 1, 2018

Acknowledgments

The idea for this book came from an internal struggle with how best to make the business case for data visualization. Data graphics are beautiful in their own right, but worthless if they cannot help you make a decision, inform your work, or communicate a finding.

I want to sincerely thank my colleagues, students, and friends for challenging me in this endeavor. While I've tried my best to mention every person that influenced this book, I apologize if I inadvertently missed someone. Know that I tried my best to recapitulate all the contributions that have formed my practice of visualizing data.

A very special thanks to Daniel Schwartz, Editor of Education at Routledge for his unwavering encouragement. He is a tremendous sponsor for my work. His constructive comments and feedback propelled my work forward and brought it to completion.

Daniel de Valk, my research assistant and former student, knows this book better than anyone else. He meticulously edited early drafts. He learned R and then set standards for how all graphs generated in R would be presented in this book. He wore many hats: editor, coder, creator, and problem solver. He spent close to a solid year of his life thinking about visualizing data, while simultaneously majoring in computer science and finance at NYU Stern School of Business.

Vishal Yadav, a talented graduate student at NYU Tandon, worked with me for over a year to build the supporting website for this book and methodically build page after page of tips, tricks, tutorials, and resources for the readers to reference. I'm indebted to Vishal for his commitment to the website and good design.

Extreme gratitude to Patricia Ahearn, who edited the final versions of the manuscript. Patricia has edited my books and articles since graduate school. I've learned much from her techniques and approach to writing.

There were over a dozen key contributors, each of whom authored an entire use case study on their practice, were interviewed as part of this book, or shared data graphics: Nicole Bohorad, Harry Chernoff, Jake Curtis, Adam Gonthier, Samantha Feldman, Andrew Hamlet, Jack

Hanlon, Reshama Shaikh, Riyaz Shaikh, Prasant Sudhakaran, Christian Theodore, Daniel de Valk, and Gregory Warwo. I am extremely grateful for the tremendous effort each of them put into crafting examples for this book.

I'm fortunate to work with remarkable colleagues at NYU Stern's W.R. Berkley Innovation Labs. They helped me to become better at communicating what it means to become visual with data. Ben Bowman brainstormed with me on various formats and the specific semantics. He helped me think about how to teach data visualization to anyone and what would be required. Cynthia Franklin read early drafts and offered valuable suggestions. Amanda Justice checked my work when it came to media formats and inspired me to think about storytelling and narrative. A special thanks to Patricia Miller, Pheobe Punzalan, and Sarah Ryan for their support and encouragement during those late nights. Luke Williams, the executive director, featured my data visualization work on NYU Stern's Ideas Never Sleep thought leadership platform and shared his overall enthusiasm for education, innovation, and good design.

Conversations with dozens of esteemed faculty members at NYU: Mor Armony, Yannis Bakos, Adam Brandenburger, Kim Corfman, Vasant Dhar, Naomi Diamant, Anyinda Ghose, Peter Henry, John Horton, Panos Ipeirotis, Srikanth Jagabathula, Natalia Levina, Hila Lifshitz-Assaf, Elizabeth Morrison, Patrick Perry, Michael Pinedo, Jan Plass, Foster Provost, Zur Shapiro, Clay Shirky, Raghu Sundaram, Arun Sundararajan, Sonny Tambe, Alex Tuzhilin, Norman White, and Eitan Zemel combined to help me understand the role of data visualization in diverse fields, the place for my book, and supported this project.

I feel honored to have learned from Stephen Chu, Amanda Cox, Hanspeter Pfister, David McCandless, Edward Tufte, and Dona Wong through their workshops and presentations. Their wisdom and practice has deeply informed my work.

Discussions with current and former NYU colleagues Jiabei Chen, Jerllin Cheng, Rachel Goldfarb, Shifra Goldenberg, Megan Hallissy, Jessy Hsieh, Roy Lee, Neil Radar, Micha Segeritz, Laura Shanley, Bob Ubell, Alanna Valdez, and Bridget Wiede provided me with new perspectives on the subject. Brainstorming sessions with Nicole Bohorad, Ted Bongiovanni, Christine Coakley, Krishan Dadlani, Kara Frantzich, Kevin Fennessey, Joseph Filani, Jo Frabetti, Thomas Guo, Esther Judelson, Akash Narendra, Nneka Penniston, Jayesh Punjaram Patil, Jason Severs, Eva Shah, Michael Sweetman, Helen Todd, and Jacqueline Yi inspired me to go further with my explanations, examples, and use cases. Also, special thanks to Jack Downey and Allyson Downey for sharing data used for some examples in this book.

This book would not be made possible without the enthusiasm of my students at NYU Stern School of Business. In particular, the Master of Science in Business Analytics students from the classes of 2014, 2015, 2016, 2017, 2018, and 2019. Thousands of students have provided me with feedback, suggestions, examples, and ideas for how best to teach and the process of visualizing data.

Finally, I have to thank my husband, Steven Goss, and my son, Penn Lee Goss, for supporting me in this project. Steven offered me critical feedback at every juncture and reinforced my reasons for writing this book. He thoughtfully commented on every chapter, case, and interview for the book. Penn made me smile every day and helped me throw the early paper drafts into the recycling bin.

Author Biography

As a leading expert on data visualization, Kristen regularly consults, delivers seminars, and leads workshops on data visualization techniques and best practices. You can find her speaking on the subject at events like Social Media Week NYC, plotly's PlotCon conference, and Tableau's events and to organizations like the National Association of Public Opinion and the National Economic Research Association.

Kristen is an associate professor of Information Systems at NYU's Stern School of Business. She teaches MBA, undergraduate, executive, and online courses in data visualization, computer programming, and the role of information technology in business and society. She is also the Director of the Learning Science Lab for NYU Stern, where she leads team to design immersive online learning environments for professional business school education.

Kristen is the co-author of *Essentials of Online Course Design: A standards-based guide* (Routledge, 2011, second edition, Routledge, 2015) and *Savvy Student's Guide to Online Learning* (Routledge, 2013). This is her third book.

Kristen received her doctorate in Communications, Computing, and Technology in Education from Columbia University. Her B.S. is from NYU Stern School of Business in Information Systems. Learn more about Kristen Sosulski at kristensosulski.com and follow her on Twitter at @sosulski.

Dr. Kristen Sosulski
Professor, Speaker, and Consultant

Contributors

HARRY G. CHERNOFF

Harry G. Chernoff is Clinical Professor of Operations Management at NYU Stern School of Business. He has been a member of the faculty of the Stern School for over 30 years. Along with having been awarded numerous honors and awards for excellence in teaching, his early teaching brought the topic of operations management to Stern and led to the development of the course and department. His business experience outside of academia is in the real estate and hospitality/gaming industries. He is an owner and developer of real estate projects in New York City, Las Vegas, and Panama City, including commercial, residential, and hotel properties. He brings much of his real estate experience from industry into the classroom.

JAKE CURTIS

Originally from Oklahoma, Jake Curtis leads sales enablement for new products on the Innovation Labs team at Return Path in New York City. He received an MBA from NYU Stern School of Business in 2018, and a B.A. in International Relations and East Asian Studies from Boston University in 2008. In his free time, he enjoys travel, speaks Mandarin Chinese, and practices yoga.

SAMANTHA FELDMAN

Sam is currently the people analytics manager at Gray Scalable, a consulting firm that provides human resources solutions to tech start-ups. In her role, she focuses on helping her clients make better HR decisions using data, primarily focusing on compensation design, talent acquisition reporting, and survey analysis. Prior to Gray Scalable, she was on the people analytics team at AOL, and she previously spent time as an HR program manager and campus recruiter. Sam holds an M.S. in Business Analytics from NYU Stern and a B.A. in Psychology from Colgate University.

ADAM GONTHIER

After years of making poorly designed data visualizations, Adam Gonthier finally learned proper visualization techniques while receiving his MBA at NYU. Adam received his Bachelor of Science degree from Lehigh University and a Master of Science degree from the University of Pennsylvania, both in Mechanical Engineering. He spent ten years in various engineering roles (R&D, manufacturing & construction) before making the move to the financial services industry after completing his MBA. Adam lives in Queens, New York with his wife and son.

ANDREW HAMLET

Andrew Hamlet is a data scientist living in Brooklyn, New York. In 2016, he correctly predicted the winners of the U.S. Primary and General Elections using social media data. Andrew graduated Phi Beta Kappa from the University of North Carolina at Chapel Hill, B.A. in Psychology, and received his MBA from NYU Stern School of Business.

JACK HANLON

As VP of Analytics, Jack is in charge of the strategy, organization, and management of the Analytics practice for Jet.com. He joined in 2015 to start up the analytics practice and customer-facing data products. In August 2016, Jet was acquired by Walmart for $3.3 billion. Prior to Jet, Jack was co-founder of Kinetic Social, a programmatic media buying and measurement platform used by brands such as Amex, Victoria's Secret, H&M, Mars, Bank of America, and Delta Airlines, among others. As a result of Kinetic's growth, he was named to the Forbes 30 Under 30. Previously, Jack worked in a variety of analytics, ML, and product-focused roles at Google and at several other eCom and Adtech startups in New York City, Boston, and San Francisco. Jack holds an M.S. from NYU and a B.A. from the College of the Holy Cross.

RESHAMA SHAIKH

Reshama is a data scientist/statistician and MBA with skills in Python, R, and SAS. She worked for over 10 years as a biostatistician in the pharmaceutical industry. She is also an organizer of the meetup group NYC Women in Machine Learning and Data Science. She received her M.S. in statistics from Rutgers University and her MBA from NYU Stern School of Business. Twitter: @reshamas

RIYAZ SHAIKH

Riyaz is a data visualization consultant. He has worked with leading startups and nonprofits, building interactive experiences and immersive visualizations. His focus is on communicating data insights through intuitive design. You can get in touch with him at riyaz@rshaikh.me

PRASANT SUDHAKARAN

Prasant is the co-founder of Aingel. Prior to co-founding Aingel, Prasant spent over 10 years in finance and consulting for firms across geographies. Starting his career as a fixed income trader, he moved on to management consulting, where he worked with multiple Fortune 500 companies, SMBs, and not-for-profit organizations. Prasant's interests lie in using Machine Learning and Artificial Intelligence in the areas of finance and marketing. He has a B.A. in Economics and Finance from De Montfort University and an M.S. in Business Analytics from New York University.

CHRISTIAN THEODORE

Christian Theodore is an independent data analyst specializing in data visualization. He is passionate about creating work that excites, engages, educates, and provokes thought in his audience. He is inspired by his multidisciplinary background in economics, international relations, psychology, and computer science, and he is hoping to make an impact on the world through information design, both as a fine art and an accessible medium for daily discourse.

GREGORY WAWRO

Gregory Wawro (Ph.D., Cornell, 1997) is a political scientist who teaches at Columbia University. He specializes in American politics (including Congress, elections, campaign finance, judicial politics, and political economy) and political methodology. He is the author of *Legislative Entrepreneurship in the U.S. House of Representatives* and co-author (with Eric Schickler) of *Filibuster: Obstruction and Lawmaking in the United States Senate*, which is a historical analysis of the causes and consequences of filibusters.

Index

Note: Page numbers in *italic* indicate figures; those in **bold** indicate tables.